Lee,

Blessings to you.

Bill Schmit

I Thess. 5:11

SHORT-HANDED

A Young Boy's Triumph over Adversity

BILL SCHULTZ

Edited by: Beth Stetenfeld

WESTBOW
P R E S S
A DIVISION OF THOMAS NELSON
& ZONDERVAN

Cover design by Linda Napiwocki

WestBow Press books may be ordered through booksellers or by contacting:

WestBow Press
A Division of Thomas Nelson & Zondervan
1663 Liberty Drive
Bloomington, IN 47403
www.westbowpress.com
1 (866) 928-1240

ISBN: 978-1-4908-2643-1 (sc)
ISBN: 978-1-4908-2644-8 (hc)
ISBN: 978-1-4908-2642-4 (e)

Library of Congress Control Number: 2014902818

Printed in the United States of America.

WestBow Press rev. date: 2/21/2014

CONTENTS

DEDICATION

To Mom:

For the love and acceptance you showed me from the moment you put your eyes on me; for the sacrifices you made so I could experience life to the fullest.

To Kathy, my beautiful wife:

For the encouragement you gave me to tell my story; for the love we share; for being my best friend.

To Brian and Bethany:

Our two great children, who are incredible blessings in my life.

To Parents of Children with Special Needs:

I hope my story, highlighting the sacrifices my parents made for me, will be an encouragement to you. My accomplishments and happiness started with acceptance and encouragement from my parents, who never underestimated my desire, determination, or abilities.

SPECIAL THANKS

To **Rachel Mathson Kleber**, for the encouragement you gave me in writing this book, and for your daily reminders to "stop working; start talking." And thank you for the hours we spent together putting thoughts on paper, and for the special person you are.

Cousin Joe, you spent many hours extracting photo images off old home movies for this book, and helped me produce video presentations. And **Cousin Midge,** who provided stories and memories about me as a small child.

Phoebe, my sister in Christ: You sat down with me one day and told me I needed to communicate my story to others and write a book about it.

Mary Creagh (Director of Public Relations at Helen Hayes Hospital) for the time spent with me, and the photographs from the hospital archives.

To my many friends, who've encouraged me throughout the process of writing this book.

INTRODUCTION

(Authors note: Jim Emery was my best friend during my grade-school years. He now lives in Savannah, Georgia, with his wife, Melissa. Jim was the first of many childhood friends who accepted me and included me in their lives.)

Schultzy,

I was very glad to hear you were writing a book about your life. I always thought you should do it. For me, you've always been a source of immense inspiration, and I suspect I'm not the only one who feels this way.

We go back a long way. We moved into the same neighborhood in Schenectady, New York during the summer of 1954. I was going into the second grade while you and my sister, Chris, were entering fourth-grade at Craig School. I remember one day when my mom suggested I go meet a guy in the neighborhood named Billy Schultz. Both my mom and yours thought we'd hit it off, and they certainly were right.

Growing up in that neighborhood was back in the "Leave it to Beaver and "Ozzie and Harriet" days. We didn't have to worry about too many things, and we just ran out and played in the neighborhood all day until we heard the dinner bell ring.

I can't really say I ever considered you "handicapped." Sure, I recognized you were different. But you certainly never acted handicapped—so I never, ever thought of you in this regard. To me, you were just a great guy. I'm not sure where you got your inner strength and courage. I'm sure some was from your folks and your older brother, but I know for sure that a lot came from Bill Schultz, himself.

I can't ever remember you feeling sorry for yourself, either. Maybe you felt this way on the inside, but you sure never let it show on the outside. There was always that laugh and chuckle and that twinkle in your eye that was your persona. I'm sure it couldn't have been easy, especially in some situations. While most guys were riding their bikes, you had to get around in your wagon or just hoof it. And maybe you couldn't climb the apple trees in the orchard like other kids, but that didn't stop you from tagging along and having a good time.

I remember the day you decided you wanted to jump off the high dive at the Edison Club pool. I remember seeing some younger kids at the pool pointing fingers at you and laughing at the "spectacle." To them, it was funny. But to me, there was nothing funny about it. It was quite simply one of the bravest and most courageous things I had seen in my life. I'll never forget it.

I'll certainly remember what a great athlete you were. Whether it was playing wiffle ball, shooting hoops and playing "horse," or golfing at the Edison Club, your athletic ability was simply amazing.

You never seemed to let anything get in your way:

- Don't have a fully functioning right leg to hit the gas pedal while driving a car? No problem. We'll just get a contraption that moves the gas pedal to the left of the brake pedal so it, too, can be used with your left foot.
- Growing fast and outgrowing your brace? No problem. We'll just solder on a new piece to add another inch to your leg.
- Can't chase down fly balls in the outfield or scamper to first base as well as other guys? No problem. We'll place Schultzy as designated pitcher and create a pinch-running situation after he smashes the baseball.

- Can't get on the Little League team? No problem. The team needs a bat boy or announcer to call the games, and who knows the players better than Bill Schultz?
- Can't make the varsity basketball team? No problem. Schultzy can be the team manager and practice his superb shooting skills on the sideline in the meantime.

While there are many things about the old neighborhood that made it a very special place to grow up, I have to say one of the greatest things was spending so much time with a kid named Bill Schultz.

All the best,
Jim Emery

ACCEPTANCE

This book is about my life journey. Given the circumstances, it could have been a story of discouragement. Instead, it's a story of encouragement from others—how they put me on a path leading to a life of fulfillment.

I was born with severe physical abnormalities that could have put significant limits on my capabilities throughout my daily life. My condition also could have affected my outlook on life—turning it negative and discouraging me from even thinking of trying. That wasn't the case.

But I could not and *did not* do it alone.

From the moment I can remember, I've always felt accepted. First, by my mom and dad—who encouraged me in all things. They helped me accept who I was and who I *could be*. They taught me discipline and never felt sorry for me. With their help, I developed a mindset that I could do anything.

I experienced similar love and encouragement from other family members: my brother, Dick; my grandmother ("Granny"); my Aunt Mickey and Uncle Teen; and my cousins, Joe and Midge. Aunt Mickey was very active in my life and showed me that my physical ability far exceeded my wildest dreams.

Throughout grade school, to junior high and high school, I was surrounded by encouraging friends. As one of friend told me years later: "We always thought you were just one of the guys." At all times, I received a healthy level of acceptance from my friends.

During my adult life, there have never been any barriers I felt I couldn't get over. Because I received a healthy level of encouragement and acceptance from the day I was born, self-confidence has helped me achieve happiness in so many ways.

I've accomplished so many things during my life:

- Playing sports in the neighborhood as a kid—baseball, basketball, and football, and learning to play golf at a high level;
- Participating on varsity teams in high school and college as a student manager;
- Singing tenor in the college glee club;
- Coaching young boys in Little League and youth basketball;
- Finding success in my business career as a sales and marketing executive, and owner of my own executive search business;
- Being actively involved in community and church activities, which has led to servant leadership opportunities and a chance to "give back;" and
- Being blessed as the husband of a beautiful woman, father of two wonderful children, and a grandfather.

Looking back on my life, I see the Lord's presence in it. He created me, accepted me, and has led me down paths only He could see. He put people in my life who've had an incredible impact on me—especially my parents and my wife, Kathy.

Not everything was easy for me. There were rough times, and periods when doubt crept into my mind.

But, ultimately, acceptance of myself and being "comfortable in my own skin" saw me through the challenges. It all started with encouragement from others throughout my life—great people who gave me strength and determination to lead a fulfilling life. My story reflects that *acceptance*.

EARLY INFLUENCERS

My immediate family was certainly the first and most influential group of people in my life.

Millicent McLaughlin—my mom, and daughter of Helena and Archibald McLaughlin—was born on Feb. 20, 1910, in the little town of Rosendale, New York.

She was the younger of two children. Her sister, Alice, whom I knew as "Aunt Mickey," was three years older. Their father, Archibald, my "Grandpa Archie," worked several different jobs in the New York City area—about 90 miles, or two hours, from their home. Their mother, Helena, my "Granny," was the first woman to become a registered nurse in Ulster County, New York but she put that career aside to raise her two daughters.

"Aunt Mickey" enjoyed doing adventurous things. Her daring and fun-loving nature ensured that she was very popular. Being late for school, going out with boys, sneaking a drink, and just having a good time were the norm for Alice.

My mom, Millicent, on the other hand, was relatively quiet and compliant, and she obeyed the rules. As the younger sister, Millicent constantly followed her older sister. Throughout their early childhood and high-school days, Alice would pull Millicent into many situations where they both got into trouble.

While Millicent was frequently nervous and fretful over it, she secretly enjoyed the independence and fun that Alice brought to her life.

Over the years, that relationship never changed. They provided healthy counterbalances for each other: They were different in many ways but always enjoyed being together.

In 1929, Millicent married **Addison Schultz** (my dad) of Kingston, New York. Millicent was only 19 years old, although women tended to marry at younger ages back then. Addison was four years older, and they had met through mutual friends.

Addison was born on July 19, 1906, in Kingston, the only child and son of Wallace and Flossy Schultz. Wallace, my "Grandpa Wally," worked for the Ulster & Delaware (U & D) Railroad, advertised as "the only all-rail route to the Catskill Mountains." Grandpa Wally was an engineer and traveled the rails extensively through southern New York.

Dad was a three-sport athlete at Kingston High School (football, basketball, and baseball). He was captain of two sports and was known for his accurate "set-shot" outside shooting in basketball. He played several positions in baseball and was one of the best athletes in the school. He played semi-professional football and became an excellent golfer later in life.

Shortly after Mom and Dad's wedding, Dad began working as a lineman with the New York Telephone Company. He worked his way up the ranks until he became a construction supervisor. That position was the reason our family moved from Kingston to Monticello, New York and eventually to Schenectady, New York, in 1953. Dad worked for the telephone company for more than 45 years.

Alice (Aunt Mickey) married Harold Clayton, also of Kingston, in 1929. I knew him as **Uncle Teen.** (Uncle Teen and Aunt Mickey were characters in a newspaper cartoon back then). It all started with Uncle Teen calling the McLaughlin house one day, wanting to ask my mom out on a date. She wasn't home and Alice answered the phone. To make a long story short, he asked Alice out and the rest is history.

Uncle Teen was a fun-loving person, too. When he graduated from high school, his father, a banker, gave him money with the option to go to college or to buy a car. Uncle Teen chose the car, although he eventually chose the path of his father and became a prominent banker in Kingston and other banks in upstate New York.

My brother, Dick, was born in 1932, thirteen years before I came into the world. My mom described him as a string bean of a kid—tall and skinny. He had his own set of challenges, suffering from asthma and bouts of eczema. Whenever I asked mom about what my brother was like when he was young, she'd describe him as "a mess" because of these maladies. Dick outgrew them in his teens and became a good high school athlete. At 6'3", he was on the high-school basketball team and played first base on the high-school baseball team. Dick also was a fine musician. In band, he played several instruments, including the cornet, trombone, and baritone. In choir, he sang tenor and had a beautiful voice.

When I was young, my brother was never around the house because of high-school sports or activities with his friends. He was involved in totally different things than I was, given the age difference. When I was three, he was 16. And, for my parents, it was like having two "only" children. I do recall sneaking into the living room several times when his girlfriend, Buzzie, came over to the house. She was a very pretty blonde, a cheerleader, a great student, and daughter of the high-school football coach. Needless to say, I was told to "get lost."

My brother, Dick, whom I admired in many ways

They eventually married in 1954, while Dick was serving in the Army. Later, they had three children—two sons (Scott and Toby) and a daughter (Diane). Dick followed in my dad's footsteps and worked at the phone company as an engineer his entire working career.

During my teenage years, I began to really know and build a relationship with my brother. He was a great role model for me—always encouraging me, and a great example as a husband and father. Dick was a friend to everyone he met, something I admired. He could strike up a conversation with anyone and make them feel comfortable. I often said to myself that, one day, I wanted to be a friend to others just like my brother. He also was the "connector" in the family—keeping in touch with relatives, and spreading the news about family happenings.

Aunt Mickey and Uncle Teen had two children, **Midge and Joe.** Cousin Midge was two years younger than my brother and became my regular baby-sitter. She walked me up and down the street we lived on, along with her good friend, Barbara Hutton.

Cousin Joe was just a year older than me, and he was like a brother. Although his interests were very different from mine, we've always been very close. Joe was very much into fixing and building things. Whenever we got together, he was building or repairing something, especially if it involved electronics. I had no idea what he was doing or how he was doing it but I enjoyed watching him put things together. Joe eventually applied his passion to become a technical education teacher for many years in the Syracuse, New York public schools.

Joe and I enjoyed doing many things together, including watching old home movies, swimming, or just spending time together and talking. For many summers, the two of us, Mom and Aunt Mickey would spend a week at a cottage on Galway Lake in upstate New York. It was a quiet lake that didn't allow motor boats. Joe and I would start fishing early in the morning to catch pickerel, and in the evening before dark to catch bass. We'd swim for many hours and dive off a raft away from shore. One year, Joe took interest in sailing and I became his boat mate. We spent hours together in this pursuit.

Cousin Joe (right), my lifelong buddy

One of our funniest moments together happened in the attic of my aunt's house. One afternoon, when we went up in the attic to play, we ended up having a fight with feather pillows. We were having a great time until we realized just about all of the feathers in the pillows were now floating in the air. When Aunt Mickey came up the stairs to see what the commotion was all about, she saw all the feathers and was not happy. We were both punished, but to this day we still laugh about it.

Throughout my early life and later, Mom was a steady influence. There was never a real high or low with her. She was a constant presence in my life. Particularly when I was a baby and a toddler, Mom had many responsibilities and challenges over and above the norm. Having a child with multiple physical disabilities, an older son to nurture and love, and the roles of wife and homemaker, gave her many challenges.

I could always count on Mom to have meals made, to drive me wherever I needed to go, and to keep the house in order. When my dad came home from work each night at 6 p.m., dinner was always on the table. Mom was a great cook and baker. Her specialties were her delicious cakes and pies. But there was one exception: filet of sole. Mom served fish every Friday, even though we weren't Catholic. Despite her efforts to make it as moist as possible, it had no taste to me. But she would always make me eat it. Much to my wife's dismay, I don't like filet of sole, or any fish, to this day!

Mom was reliable, and concerned that things be done the "right" way. She rarely ventured into trying new things. But when I was growing up, I could always count on my mom to have certain things done and to be there when I needed her. I always knew what she expected, she gave me limits, and she taught me what I should and shouldn't do in most situations.

SPECIAL DELIVERY

(Note: The preceding chapters set the stage for my entrance into the world, and provide a brief picture of the major characters who preceded me and helped shape my life. When I was born, they provided support and encouragement, and helped me overcome the many obstacles I would face.

The year I was born, 1945, was an eventful year for the U.S. World War II was coming to a successful end—with Germany surrendering in July, shortly after Hitler committed suicide, and Japan surrendering in September. President Franklin Roosevelt died in office that year, and Vice President Harry Truman became president. The U.S. dropped atomic bombs on Hiroshima and Nagasaki.

At home, the popular toys were erector sets, electric trains, Silly Putty, and the Slinky. Popular radio shows included "The Lone Ranger," "The Jimmy Durante Show," and "The Shadow." New housing developments began to spring up in the suburbs.

On July 23rd of that year, in upstate New York, Millicent Schultz was in the ninth month of her pregnancy, anxiously awaiting the birth of her second child. Her first child, Dick, a few months shy of 13 years old, was off playing with his school buddies. Her husband, Addison, was at work at the New York Telephone Company, but stayed close to his phone anticipating a call from her at any moment. It was a typical warm summer day, and she felt healthy and very excited about her new baby.

That morning, her water broke, and her husband and sister accompanied her to the hospital. The nurses and doctors moved her into a delivery room. A few hours later, her contractions came sooner and harder and her new baby boy, later named Billy, was born. Like any post-delivery, the baby was wheeled away, placed in a warmer, and examined by the doctors.

In the 1940s, laboring women were routinely sedated shortly before delivery, and babies commonly were delivered from their unconscious mothers with forceps. The sedation had its effect for a short time after the birth. As Mom's sedative began to wear off, she sensed that something was wrong. She noticed the hospital attendants' and nurses' attitudes toward her were strange. She kept asking them to "bring me my baby." No one would say anything to her, and they kept her waiting. Finally, in the afternoon, after she had kept after them all day, the doctor, her husband, and her sister told her the reason: Billy was deformed.

The doctors discovered I had multiple congenital deformities. The biggest abnormality was the incomplete formation of my right femur—the bone from the hip to the knee, or the thigh bone. As a result, my right leg was significantly shorter than my left. In addition, the toes of my left foot were fused together.

The other major deformity involved my left arm and hand. In layman's terms, my left forearm—between the elbow and the wrist—was incomplete, smaller, and shorter, and my left hand was incomplete, considerably smaller, and shorter than normal, with only a small thumb and two tiny fingers attached. My left arm was about half the length of my right arm.

When the time came for Mom to put her eyes on her new son, a nurse unwrapped her baby from the blanket. When Mom saw me for first time, she looked past the physical deformities and focused on her little baby's eyes. When she caught sight of that 'darling little face,' she knew she could accept the rest. As the days went by and Mom had time to collect her thoughts, she quickly became determined that Billy Schultz would be raised as a normal child and accepted as such.

That was the positive attitude my mom had from the very beginning—an attitude mirrored and reinforced by my dad, her sister (Aunt Mickey), her mother (Granny), and her close friends. From the beginning, Aunt Mickey was her constant companion and helper.

We've never found a definitive explanation for the cause of the deformities. A bilateral (affecting both an arm and a leg) deformity is rare. My mom did contract German measles very early in the pregnancy, and that might have been the cause. But the doctors weren't sure. Mom did not take any drugs during the pregnancy, not even for pain relief.

But the cause didn't matter to mom. She didn't dwell on the why or the wherefore. She was determined to make me feel loved and accepted.

Right from the start, I was surrounded by people—starting with Mom and Dad—who encouraged me and helped me tackle and overcome many obstacles. As they took me home from the hospital, my parents faced unique challenges, obstacles, and decisions. Many of my needs were quite apparent and required immediate attention. Mom and Dad were in "uncharted waters."

A WHOLE NEW WORLD

A few years before I was born, my parents had bought a new home in Kingston. It was a two-story, white colonial house, with nice back and front yards, a large living room, and a big bay window in the dining room.

At the age of one, when many toddlers begin to walk, crawling was my method. I didn't have any other way of getting around. Mom told me I would try to get up on my one leg with the natural instinct of wanting to take a step. But, of course, when I tried it I'd tumble to the floor. I had no crutches, and I was still too young to be fitted for an artificial leg. I didn't crawl headfirst like most babies do, because my left arm was half as long as my right. I discovered I could get around by crawling sideways, with my left leg in front of me and my right hand behind my body, pushing me forward. As I got older, in a similar way, I would use the heel on my left shoe to help me move forward. It was hard at first, but that method help me scoot—the faster the better.

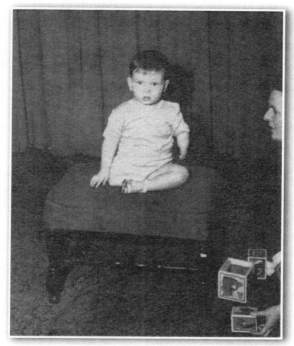

Me, being photographed at the age of one, with Mom looking on

I was literally a "rug rat." Mom said I tried every day to get faster—moving around the house, whether it was crawling down the hallways to the bedrooms or scooting to the front of the house to the living room. The carpets in our house were very thin with no padding underneath. I crawled so much I began to create noticeable paths in the carpets. Our house was small, so there wasn't much carpeting to maneuver.

Crawling became a real game for me, and it seemed like I did it every waking moment of my early life. It was such a simple thing, but it was a source of childhood joy and fun. In my world, for longer than most children, I looked up at everything. And all objects and people looked so large and tall. I'm sure I crawled around my mother's feet many times, wondering what she was doing at the time. Usually, it was cooking or cleaning or altering my clothes. I made a game of it—trying to get around the house faster and faster, down the hallway to the bedrooms or off to the living room. I regularly wore out my pants. I can't imagine the number of pairs I went through, but it certainly kept my mom continually sewing to keep up.

On many occasions, I sat on a bench seat looking out the bay window—watching kids playing, Dad mowing the lawn, or Dad coming home from work. I'd gaze across the street at a "huge" corn field, which was the garden of our neighbor, Mr. Kias, the high-school athletic director. My world was expanding.

As I grew a little taller and my one good leg got stronger, I began to realize I could prop myself up, stand, and lean against a wall. To grip any object—like a chair arm or a furniture post—to raise my body, only my right hand could help me. For a time, when I tried that, I'd fall right down on my back or on my face. I'd cry, but like a new baby who's learning to walk, I'd get up and try again and again.

As my left leg got strong enough to support me, I found another way to adapt: I learned how to hop! Of course I fell down many times, much to the chagrin of my mother. But instead of sheltering me, as she probably would have liked to have done, she let me keep trying.

So I graduated from the school of scooting to the school of hopping, although the pratfalls continued. I got around a little faster, and I began to focus on things that were three feet taller or higher. The Lord blessed me with a tremendous sense of balance, which made hopping an effective way to get around. I made a game of standing on my left leg, not holding anything with my hands, for as long as I could.

In the house, Mom usually had music playing on the radio during the day as she did her chores. One day when I was still quite young, she heard me trying to sing along with the songs on the radio. I continued to do that for a few days and she soon realized the enjoyment I found in singing. She also realized I could sing on key.

A few days later, Mom came into the living room where I was playing. She put a box in front of me and plugged an attached electrical cord into the wall socket. She opened the lid of the box to show me a Victrola—a small phonograph record player that played 10-inch vinyl records. She bought a couple of records just for me. I immediately enjoyed listening to and singing along with this new source of music.

I spent many hours sitting on the living room floor—playing records and singing along.

My cousin Midge later told me that every time she came to visit I was sitting by the Victrola—singing along to whatever record was playing. Mom, early on, recognized my ear for and interest in music and singing, which have been lifelong joys. That early exposure to music also opened up many great opportunities for me later in life.

Music also was a joy to my mom who, herself, sang in the church choir, played the piano, and later learned to play the organ.

Crawling, hopping, singing, peering out the window—I was discovering all kinds of new things to do and enjoy.

DECISIONS, DECISIONS

As my parents brought me home from the hospital, they had numerous questions and concerns to address. How would my physical disabilities affect my daily life and life in general? How would I function and, in particular, how would I learn to walk? Significant time and medical costs would be needed. They'd have to meet with orthopedic doctors to determine a course of action—leading to probable surgery and therapy.

As a parent, I can't imagine how overwhelmed and emotional my parents must have been. As they first looked at me in my bassinet, the questions on their minds must have overwhelmed them: How do we help our child? What do we do next? Will our young boy ever be able to walk? If he's able to walk, will he be severely limited in what he can do? How will we handle all the special needs he'll have as he grows up? How can we get him the proper medical attention, and how can we pay for it?

They also needed encouragement and emotional support, as there were many times when they felt overwhelmed and ill-equipped. The whispers of neighbors and the sympathies of friends, even lacking ill intentions, didn't help. Comments such as, "Poor Millicent" and "What a shame about the baby," were overheard many times.

The main person who carried the biggest part of this burden was my mom. Dad was at work every day as the provider for the family. Mom was the one who had to think about all these questions day after day. I'm sure there were days when she'd break down and cry and ask why this happened to her little child. I'm sure there were moments when she felt guilty—perhaps feeling that she'd done something wrong during the pregnancy.

In later years, I found a box she'd filled with notes and articles she'd collected. One was a newspaper article written by a medical doctor, titled, "Infant Malformations Not Fault of Parents." The doctor encouraged mothers of handicapped children not to carry a burden of guilt. His article pointed out many factors beyond the control of a pregnant mother that could cause deformity, such as German measles or other diseases. In fact, the article described, "Many children with in-born malformations rise to heights of fame or national acclaim, which speaks well for the ability of human beings to overcome adversity." The fact that Mom kept that article could mean she felt guilty at times. But it also could also have been an encouragement to her. Her child had the potential to face life challenges successfully.

Because I was born with a congenital and severe deformity of my right leg and hip joint, the orthopedists my parents consulted initially had to determine the extent of the deformity, and whether any further amputation was necessary. My right thigh bone, or femur, was partially formed and incomplete. There was a small foot attached to the end of the incomplete femur. Functionally, the foot was useless. The orthopedists recommended that the foot be amputated and that what was left of the incomplete femur be retained. The plan was to amputate near where the hip joint should be, without cutting the bone, and to form a "stump," so I could eventually be fitted for a leg I'd be able to walk on.

The initial artificial leg they had in mind could best be described as a "peg leg." My stump would fit into a socket (or bucket), which was attached to a metal rod with a curved rubber bumper at the end. The bumper touched the ground. A leather belt, extending around my waist, would hold the leg on to my body. No matter how much reassurance the doctors gave my parents about a positive outcome, it must have been emotionally draining and scary for them to think about surgery on their 1 ½-year-old child. I imagine them thinking, "Will it work?" "Will he be able to walk on just a peg...a metal rod?" "Could he hurt himself?"

The next hurdle for my parents was figuring how to make the necessary surgery affordable and making sure the surgery was performed by doctors who'd already performed similar procedures. They also knew it was critical for me to have physical therapy after the surgery to learn how to walk.

In the fall of 1946, through discussions with doctors and therapists, they were referred to case managers from the state of New York to determine their next course of action. Mom and Dad needed financial support to provide me with the best care available at that time. Fortunately, New York State provided financial and medical resources to help parents facing major medical procedures or long-term care for their children—resources my parents needed to ensure the best outcome for me.

The state case managers referred my parents to doctors at the New York State Reconstruction Hospital for Children (what a terrible name). Later, this hospital was renamed the New York State Rehabilitation Hospital, and it's now known as the Helen Hayes Hospital. This is where the surgery would be performed and the necessary therapy would take place. The hospital was located in Haverstraw, New York, 60 miles from our home in Kingston and an hour's drive north of New York City.

Aerial view of New York State Reconstruction Hospital for Children (Haverstraw, New York, circa 1950)

This hospital was the nation's first free-standing, state-operated hospital dedicated to the treatment of children with physical disabilities. It initially was established in 1900 to provide treatment to children suffering from tuberculosis, which was a public health epidemic at that time. In the 1940s and early '50s, the leading causes of hospitalization at the facility were polio and congenital physical deformities of children. Children treated at the facility ranged in age from toddlers to teenagers. Because lengths of stay ranged from several months to many years, the hospital had a K-12 school on the grounds, which the children attended when they weren't being treated. The campus was huge—with many wings off the main building and the hospital grounds extending down to the banks of the Hudson River.

In February 1947, my parents drove me to Haverstraw from our home in Kingston to have the necessary surgery performed at the hospital. They were told that after the surgery, I'd have to stay at the hospital while the amputation properly healed. Evaluation would follow, to make sure the newly formed stump would properly fit into the socket of the new leg. Each day of my eventual physical therapy, I'd need to spend hours working with therapists—learning how to walk with my new peg leg. The doctors told my parents my stay at the hospital would last about six months—for the newly formed stump to heal properly and to provide the needed physical therapy and training to learn how to walk.

Mom was able to stay with me during and after the surgery, which went about as well as expected. But eventually she had to return home to Kingston. Dad was back at work, and my brother Dick was attending high school. The hospital was so far away—about 1 ½ hours by car. Since they had only one car, which my dad used for work, visiting me was difficult. My family came to visit me every weekend on Sunday— visiting day at the hospital. Communication with the hospital and the doctors could only be done by phone, and it was quite hard to get in touch with them.

Mom with me at the hospital in Haverstraw (summer of 1947)

Back at the hospital, I was learning how to walk. Until now, I'd never taken a natural step. Crawling had been my main mode of moving around. Since I was without a hip joint to help swing the artificial limb, it wasn't easy to learn to walk properly. Hours of walking with a prototype peg leg followed. I had to adapt my natural instincts for walking with my left leg and learn new ways of walking with my new right peg leg.

Of course there were many falls and scrapes as I learned to walk. One tool the therapists used was a "Humpty Dumpty" puzzle. They asked me to walk to the other side of a room and bring a puzzle piece back to the puzzle board. After months of therapy, in the words of the therapists, I "took off."

With the exception of the time with the therapists, I spent the rest of my time in a hospital bed or in a wooden wheelchair. I was in a hospital ward occupied by at least a dozen young children with several beds on each side and an aisle in the middle. It must have been a noisy ward! There were no televisions or radios—just the noises of the other kids, and the voices of the nurses or doctors. It made for a long and lonely six-month hospital stay.

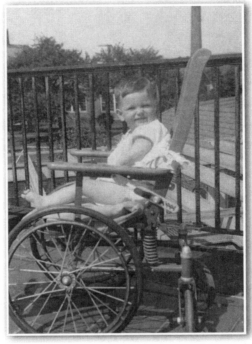

In my wooden wheelchair, outside on the hospital patio (spring of 1947)

I was released from the hospital in late August 1947—shortly after my second birthday. I'm sure it was one of the happiest days for my parents (and an even happier day for me) when they took me home.

I certainly can't recall any particular experiences at that age. But the fact that, for six months, I wasn't interacting much with other children my age or with other people besides therapists and nurses must have weighed heavily on my parents. Did we do the right thing? How would that long stay affect their son? Did he fall behind developmentally?

During those long months of separation, I imagine my mom woke every morning and thought, "I want to be with my little boy."

Mom told me years later it was one of the most difficult days of her life to leave me at a hospital far away from home. She cried all the way home after they left me and for many days afterward. I'm sure it was upsetting to dad, too, but he was the type of person who internalized emotions. Can you imagine, as a parent, not seeing or being with your toddler for weeks on end? It must have been an unbearable and highly emotional time for them. After becoming a parent and grandparent, myself, when I think back on that experience it makes me realize the impact it must have had on my parents as they drove away from the hospital, knowing my stay at Haverstraw would be six long months!

While the ordeal was extremely difficult, my parents understood how important it was for me to have the surgery and to get the necessary training to learn how to walk using an artificial leg. I was too young to recall the emotional pain, but I'm certain I cried like any baby separated from his parents. Thinking about the impact this experience would have on me must have caused my parents to feel guilt and sadness. But what was important to them was that they knew it was the right thing to do for me. It was such a selfless act on their part.

One individual played a very positive role in our lives during this time: a local car dealer. He'd heard of my long stay in the hospital and the fact that my mom didn't have a car to drive and visit me. One day, he knocked on our door, and when my mom opened it, he introduced himself with a big smile. He handed her a set of car keys and said he hoped she could go visit her son when she wanted and needed to do so. The car parked outside was hers to use and to keep—no strings attached.

I can only imagine the shock, and then the smile, on Mom's face.

THE NEXT STEPS

In 1948, a year after I returned home from the hospital, the next challenge for my parents was to find a prosthetist (or brace-maker, as I called them, because it was much easier to pronounce). The brace-maker would design, fabricate, and fit me with a new peg leg that could be adjusted in length as I grew taller.

I remember traveling with my folks to visit my first brace-maker, who lived and worked in the Catskill Mountains, about an hour from our home. My parents were quite surprised to discover that this individual worked and lived in a log cabin. They wondered whether they should even go up to the door. Since we'd traveled so far, they decided to meet with the man.

I remember him greeting us at the door. I recall seeing a big man with a dark beard and a wide smile. I remember a large living room area, filled with deer-head trophies on the walls and the warm scent of an open fireplace. The man welcomed us in and the three adults discussed my story. To my parents' relief, they realized this brace-maker could design and fit me with a peg leg similar to the one I'd trained on at the hospital. He would be able to lengthen the new leg as I grew taller.

The man spent a few months designing and making the leg, and I was almost three years old when I returned to his home and walked on it for the first time. It felt similar to my first leg. And when he and my parents saw me successfully walking with it, I could see the smiles (and relief) on their faces.

Walking with my new peg leg (at age 3)

We had now overcome one major hurdle in my ability to walk, and my life was about to become very active. For the next four years, my peg leg and I were "joined at the hip." I was ready to take off.

My new peg leg allowed me to experience life from new perspectives. Now, in addition to crawling and hopping, I could walk quite well. Though I was now three, I was like a one-year-old learning how to walk and explore for the first time. Like a caged dog, when released, I took off—fast.

My brother and my cousins later told me I smiled constantly as I became more and more active. For me, it was like opening a Christmas present. My mom described how I was constantly on the move and how I loved to be outside just walking around, up and down the driveway. I was determined and eager to try everything. I enjoyed any game or activity that included a ball. I was born with a love for sports.

My parents got me a short, plastic golf club that I began swinging at the age of three. I also began throwing a tennis ball around the yard, not always to someone else. It was very awkward, at first, to throw a ball and maintain my balance. As soon as I released the ball, I'd fall down during my follow through. I'd throw it as far as I could, retrieve it, and then throw it again and again until I was exhausted. But my confidence grew.

Playing with my plastic golf club in the front yard

My dad was amazed at how straight I could throw a ball. Much to Mom's chagrin, I kicked a rubber ball constantly inside the house— from one room to another, like I was in a kickball game. We had a black cocker spaniel, named Topsy, who was my playmate, chasing after whatever ball I was playing with at any time, both inside the house and in the yard. I had a natural urge to run, and I learned the hard way that running on a peg leg wasn't the easiest thing to do. My good leg was usually way ahead of my peg leg, and many times I fell to the ground, usually on my face, my elbow, or my shoulder. Uneven ground sometimes tripped me up, even when I was simply walking. But I was determined to run and do what I wanted, and I soon adapted.

I'm sure my mom was scared whenever I went outside. She easily could have justified keeping me inside the house. But I think she saw the joy in my face and the fun I was having when she gave me freedom. She encouraged me to try new things, even when at first I failed. She didn't overprotect me, even though that was her first instinct. She encouraged me to try and try again—an attitude I've carried all my life.

Because of my extended stay at the hospital, and my delayed adjustments as a toddler, I wasn't able to interact with other kids my age. Mom had many friends whose children were older or lived a few miles away. When I came home from the hospital, my brother Dick was 15 and involved in high-school activities. I rarely saw him. Fortunately, Aunt Mickey and Uncle Teen, and cousins Midge and Joe, lived only a couple of blocks away, literally around the corner and up the hill.

But even though I got around fairly well with my peg leg, it was difficult for me to keep up with other kids in the neighborhood. As a result, I spent a lot of time alone playing inside or outside the house. When inside, I sometimes took off my peg leg and got back to scooting and hopping—a much faster way to move around. I became a master of the art of hopping. I made a game of it—trying to hop more times without holding anything, and to hop as high and as fast as I could. The sound of my hopping around the house probably bothered my mom and made her nervous, but she never stopped me from doing it. Most days, when the weather allowed it, I went outside, hopped on the front lawn, and then tried, failed, and succeeded in hopping around to the back lawn, and back to the front again. The unevenness of the lawn made it challenging, and I guess that's what made it fun.

Around my fourth birthday, Mom and Dad decided to buy me a tricycle. With two wheels in back and one in front, it seemed sturdy and balanced, and unlikely to tip over easily. Other kids were riding them around the neighborhood. My parents had seen the level of body control and coordination that I had playing ball and walking around the house. However, I would have to take off my peg leg to ride it, and they didn't know how I'd feel about that. They went ahead and bought one, anyway. They showed it to me and explained I'd have to ride it without my peg leg. I'd seen other kids ride their trikes and bikes up and down the street and it looked like so much fun. I was so excited to do what other kids were doing that taking my leg off was a no-brainer. I couldn't wait to try it.

Riding on my new tricycle

Mom and Dad warned me to ignore any remarks or questions from neighborhood kids. Frankly, I didn't even think or care what other kids might say. I was so excited to be able to ride. My parents restricted me to riding it only on our driveway to get used to it. It wasn't very long before I was riding my trike up and down the driveway for hours. My dad finally took me out along our street to show me where I could ride safely. Our street, Madison Avenue, was a straight side street that dead-ended at a National Guard Armory. It was quiet and safe. Still, Dad "struck fear" in me, describing cars running into people and hurting them badly. I made certain I followed his instructions, and I always rode near the side of the street.

As my confidence grew, though, I ventured further down the street toward the Armory, which was visible from our front lawn. It took me a long time to get to that end of the street, but it was only about a hundred yards from our house. I'm pretty sure my parents didn't want me to ride that far, and I always looked back at our house to see if Mom was outside looking for me. But venturing out that far came to a halt when, one day, as I looked back, I saw a large snake climbing up the back of my tricycle. To a five-year old, that snake looked enormous, and I was never so scared in my life. I imagined myself getting bitten and dying! I quickly turned around and peddled with my left leg as fast as I could to get back home. Halfway there, I could see the snake crawling up the trike and getting closer to the seat. I jumped off my trike, fell to the ground, and hopped the rest of the way. I was never so happy to get home and hug my mom.

I stuck closer to home after that. I'm sure I was foolish to think that Mom didn't know where I'd been. I'm sure she did and it probably worried her, but this was yet another example of her letting me try and explore new experiences.

I was also curious about the cornfield across the street. It looked like a great place to hide or simply explore. One day, I decided to ditch the trike and hop into the cornfield. Once inside the rows of corn, I got on my hands and knees and started crawling—actually scooting, like I did inside our house. I was having a great time until I realized how muddy my clothes were. And my hands were black with dirt. I realized I'd lost my sense of direction and had no idea how to get out! Soon, I heard Mom calling for me. The good news: Her calls told me the direction in which to crawl to find my way out. The bad news: I faced Mom as I reappeared, very dirty from head to toe. As she looked down at me, she simply shook her head at her brown mess of a kid. She didn't say a word, and none were needed. I don't recall making a return visit to the cornfield.

In 1949, when I was four, my parents faced another challenge in my development. It was time to train for school and to learn to associate with other children. Since there were no nursery schools in Kingston, Mom and Dad took me to St. Ursula School, a convent school for girls, run by the Sisters of St. Ursula. There were a few other boys there, too, but the goal of this Catholic order was to teach girls who didn't have the educational opportunities available to boys. It was located in a two-story house with a wrap-around porch. The rooms were small, with 10-15 students in each. French nuns operated the convent, and although our family was Protestant, this made no difference. The nuns were especially kind and interested in helping me prepare for public school. Mom was very appreciative. She told me I learned many Christmas carols in Latin, learned a bit of French, and wondered why my teacher "wore her coat all day." The nuns were very fond of me, and told my mom many times that I would be a "good Catholic."

After that, I attended kindergarten and part of first grade at a public school in Kingston. I remember school days when kids stared at my peg leg and my short arm and hand, and other kids followed me down the hall, or gave me funny looks. I had to sit at my desk with my peg leg extended out to the side because I couldn't bend it. The stares bothered me and I didn't quite understand why some kids stared a lot. My parents told me to always expect comments and stares because I was different physically from most children.

As they got to know me, and saw how physically active and friendly I was, most of the kids accepted me. Of course, there were kids who continued to make comments about me and who laughed and stared at my peg leg and hand. It hurt to be the center of attention simply because of my physical differences, but I had to learn how to deal with it. The fact that I was accepted by many of my classmates helped me realize that just being myself was good enough for them to be friends.

Ultimately, I trace my attitude back to how Mom and Dad raised me. From the day I was born, my parents were committed to raising me like a normal child as much as possible. They loved me and accepted me at all times, but they didn't coddle or overprotect me. They allowed me to try, and try again—whether it was singing along with the Victrola, crawling or hopping on the rug, swinging my plastic golf club, running outside, throwing balls around the yard, riding my tricycle, or just exploring things a typical young boy would do.

They knew I'd fall and stumble, which happened many times. I often came into the house with tears in my eyes and scrapes on my elbows, but they encouraged me to get up and try again. Eventually, their encouragement produced my own desire and determination to try and succeed at many endeavors. But they also disciplined me when I misbehaved, including when I ventured too far from home or wandered away—like I had in the cornfield. They didn't give me any slack, and they disciplined me the same way they'd disciplined my brother.

I'm sure Mom shed worried tears many days, as she saw me try activities that scared her. The thought of me hurting myself was always on her mind. Should she let me try each new activity?

She and my dad knew the extent of my physical disabilities. But they didn't know what I could, or couldn't, do until they let me try. They couldn't measure my determination, and they didn't want to discourage me. They gave me the gift of the attitude to try—that was their greatest gift. I often failed—when trying to climb a tree, going up stairs without using the hand rail, or keeping up with kids running in the neighborhood. But I often succeeded. And by trying, I began to build a healthy level of self-confidence and a positive attitude—both of which have stayed with me my entire life.

RETURN TO HAVERSTRAW

In the fall of 1951, my dad earned a promotion at the phone company, requiring us to move to Monticello, New York, about 60 miles from Kingston. My parents sold their house quickly and found a new home in Monticello, which we moved into shortly before Christmas. I remember that because when we all walked through the front door on moving day, there in the living room was our first television set—a "housewarming" gift from Dad. I remember letting out a big yell when I saw it. I was excited about getting presents because it was Christmastime, and it took my mind off missing my neighborhood friends back in Kingston.

My parents—in addition to preparing to move, saying goodbye to their many friends, and registering me for my second semester of first grade—faced another decision. Since age three, I'd been getting around on my peg leg, having it adjusted for my increasing height. Now I was six, and they realized they needed to consider alternatives to help me walk better. Since the end of World War II, in 1945, many veterans had returned home in need of artificial limbs as a result of their war injuries. This increased demand resulted in new prosthetic limb clinics and advances in limb design.

While I was adjusting to my new school in the early months of 1952, case managers once again referred my parents back to the Haverstraw hospital. The facility had expanded its prosthetics lab, where it designed and manufactured limbs with improved functionality and cosmetic appearance. My parents decided I should be admitted to the hospital after the school year to have a fully functional leg designed for me. I'd stay at the hospital, again, to be fully fitted for the new leg and trained to walk on it.

I was unaware of any of this planning. I had my own concerns and questions about my new school and neighborhood: Will I be accepted by the kids? Will I be able to make new friends? Will I be able to play outside? Are there any other kids in the neighborhood I can play with?

Our house in Monticello was at the top of a hill, with the nearest house at the bottom of it. We could see only a few other houses in the distance. Since we moved during the winter, I was inside the house for the first few months. I enjoyed our new TV and watching kids' shows like "Howdy Doody" and cartoons for the first time. We lived close enough to New York City to pick up several stations.

I remember my mom talking about an entertainer by the name of Peg Leg Bates who performed regularly on a local television show each Saturday morning. As his name implies, he had one good leg and a peg leg—the result of a cotton gin accident at the age of 12. My mom encouraged me to watch the show. He'd taught himself how to be an amazing tap dancer, and he flew around the stage with incredible ease and with joy on his face. It inspired me to see someone else with a peg leg so active and so happy. Peg Leg Bates became a nationally known entertainer, and danced until the age of 96.

When spring arrived in Monticello, I looked forward to playing outside. It was difficult to get down our steep hill to play in the street, but even more challenging to get back up. I figured it out, but not without some scraped knees and ripped pants in the process. Fortunately, we had a large, level backyard. It looked huge to me, and there was an open field behind it, as well. The yard was great for playing any game involving a ball or running. I had mastered the art of running on my peg leg and kept trying to run faster, in spite of several pratfalls.

I don't recall any close friendships because we lived in Monticello for a very short time. I attended the second half of first grade and a short part of second grade there. I was very young and rarely invited kids from my class over to play. I was used to playing by myself, but I missed playing with other kids as I had in our old neighborhood. Cousin Joe visited once in a while but it was a long trip from their new residence in Rome, New York.

When the school year came to a close, Mom and Dad sat me down and explained to me how important it was for me to be fitted for a new and improved artificial leg. They told me how it would allow me to walk better and get around much easier; how I'd have increased mobility with less physical effort.

With my stiff peg leg, I had to sit on the right side of any chair—by straddling the seat to allow the peg leg to touch the floor. If I was inside at home, I'd usually take the leg off so I could sit more comfortably and move around easier. Mom and Dad said that with the new leg design, I'd be able to sit normally on a chair, like the rest of the kids, and that I could unlock and bend the leg at the hip and the knee. My right pant leg would collapse around the metal rod. With the new leg, my right leg would now be shaped like my left one, a great improvement, physically and cosmetically.

It all sounded exciting to me. But then they told me something else—I had to return to the hospital in Haverstraw.

Though I had little recollection of that first experience, because I'd been only two at the time, I wasn't happy about returning. Mom showed me pictures—of me sitting outside the hospital in a wheelchair, or sitting on a bed with a smile on my face. But I didn't like the thought of going into a hospital in the summertime. I'd been looking forward to playing and running and having fun. I let my parents know I wasn't happy about it, but they helped me realize how important this return visit would be for me.

In July 1952, we took the one-hour trip to the hospital. I remember sitting in the front seat—between Mom and Dad—and feeling very sad thinking about being away from them. I distinctly remember the disappointment of looking through the front window and seeing a road sign for the Haverstraw exit. I began to cry uncontrollably, holding on to Mom, and hoping she'd say I didn't have to go, that we could go home.

Mom held me tight, and she looked just as sad. As we drove up to the front door, I knew I would not be going home for a while.

I recall sitting with my parents as they filled out all the necessary forms. I sat very quietly, not knowing what to expect or how long I'd be there. It seemed like an hour, yet I'm sure it was only a few minutes. The admissions person directed my parents to the ward where I'd be staying. As we walked down a narrow, dark hall, I held Mom's hand tightly not wanting to let go.

My ward had two rows of 16 beds each, with a wide aisle in the middle. Glass partitions separated every two beds. The ward looked long and endless, and was stark white. Every bed was taken except one near the far end. As we walked down the aisle past each set of beds, we were met with stares and some comments. When we reached my bed, a nurse arrived to talk with us. But I didn't hear a word. My mind was off thinking about home, playing in the backyard, and having fun.

The next thing that happened made me feel even worse. Mom asked me to take off my peg leg. I looked at her, not understanding what she'd just said. It didn't really hit me until she told me I'd never wear it again—I'd be learning how to walk with a different leg. The prosthetics people, she said, would help me walk on prototypes that would have an entirely different "feel." I began to cry again and looked at her, asking "Why?" She explained that "for a little while" I'd be getting around in a wheelchair. I didn't understand. I was never so sad in my life—too sad to even scream or pull a temper tantrum. She talked to me again about the new leg and how it would help me, but her words didn't make me feel any better. All I could think about was being in a bed or a wheelchair all day.

My hospital ward during my second stay at Haverstraw (1952)

The lowest point in my life came next. My parents had to say goodbye and head home. Mom began to cry and I joined in. I held on to her, not wanting to let go. Dad's face was down, hiding his emotions. As they walked away down that long aisle in the ward, I strained my neck out, not wanting to lose sight of them.

As they disappeared, I felt like the loneliest person in the world.

Here I was lying in a bed, unable to walk, in a room filled with other children I didn't know. I didn't want to be there. I was confined and didn't what was going to happen to me.

I fell asleep, exhausted. When I awoke, I began looking around and making eye contact with the other kids. They looked at me from their beds with curiosity. A couple of the older kids came by in their wheelchairs. Many were like me, with some congenital physical deformity. About half of them were at the hospital because they'd contracted polio, a scourge for many children in the late '40s and early '50s. Some polio patients lay flat in their beds with limited body movement due to paralysis. Others with even more severe cases were encased in a device called an "iron lung"—a tank respirator used on acute cases when a patient had difficulty breathing because the polio virus paralyzed his or her chest muscles. Only the patient's head was outside the tank. The sight of an iron lung scared me. I could see loneliness and sadness in the children's eyes.

Overall, the ward was unusually quiet, with some outbursts of laughter or crying. The routine was the same every day. The nurses woke us, cleaned up, served our meals, and wheeled us individually to our various appointments or to school during the day. In my case, those trips were usually to the prosthetics area, two or three times a week. About half our waking hours were spent sitting on our beds. Whenever a nurse came in to wheel one of us away, we'd go the ends of our beds and watch.

One of my daily habits was reclining on my back, watching the large ceiling fans circling slowly and constantly. The beds in the ward were too far away from each other for us to talk without raising our voices.

We were in our own little worlds. On many days, I wondered why I was there. Was this all worth it? Would I ever get out?

My section mate was another little boy, named Sammy. He was being treated for polio and he rarely spoke. I tried to talk to him, but I rarely got a response. During the time I was there, he had no visitors. I never knew why. He just sat in his bed looking out in space. When my mom came to visit me, she'd spend time with Sammy, just talking to him and rubbing his hand. Occasionally, he'd give her a brief smile.

The hospital buildings were extensive—connected by long, winding, hallways with brick walls, leading to the prosthetics area, pool, school, auditorium, and everything else. I remember being wheeled each day to some of these areas. My eyes looked out each window I passed, and I thought about how great it would be to be outside playing again.

The days blended together. Mom left me with some books to read and blank pads for drawing. I don't recall where we ate our meals; I believe they were brought to us. The nurses helped us take baths and keep ourselves clean. On nice weather days, they'd wheel us out to sit on the lawns or outside patios. The lawns surrounding the hospital were expansive.

Occasionally we'd have picnics outside, with all the children gathered on the same area of the lawn. The nurses and other hospital staff joined us and visited with us. Even at the age of seven, I appreciated the beautiful scenery. It was just nice to be out in the fresh air, talking to people—even adults! I had this ongoing urge to get out of the wheelchair and hop around or crawl on the ground. I dreamed of hopping across the large lawn until I was exhausted. I so missed running and playing. I felt very confined.

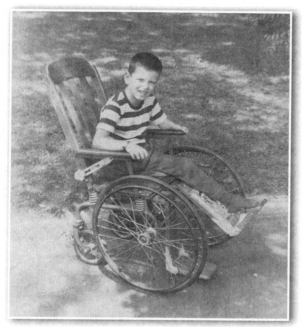

In my wheelchair, outside on the hospital lawn (July, 1952)

By wearing a life preserver vest, I was able to use the hospital's pool. I remember workers bringing polio victims to the pool and carrying them in the water. Seeing their limp bodies, I felt fortunate to be able to swim on my own. I tried to stay in the pool as long as possible, because I enjoyed it and because the alternative was going back to the ward.

But all of us looked forward to Friday nights, when we watched black-and-white movies—usually Westerns. Popular cowboy heroes included Red Ryder, Hopalong Cassidy, and Gene Autry. The nurses wheeled us down to a large auditorium. They used gurneys instead of wheelchairs because most of the kids couldn't sit up. The room was always full—wall-to-wall—with kids on gurneys looking at a movie screen. Those nights got really noisy, and the movies took our minds off of ourselves.

One night, when we returned to the ward, I was "wound up" after watching one of the movies. When it was time for bed, the nurses turned out the lights. That night, I couldn't sleep and I began talking to other kids and laughing to myself. All of a sudden a light at the end of the ward turned on and a nurse appeared. She quickly walked down the aisle toward my bed. I thought she was only going to talk to me and tell me to be quiet. Instead, she grabbed a gurney near my bed and told me to get on it. The next thing I knew I was headed out of the ward, on the gurney, to a dark room with a very dim light. She told me I'd be sleeping there that night, and she shut the door. I was so scared, I cried myself to sleep.

Fortunately, there were days to look forward to—like Sundays. Visiting hours were in the afternoon, when parents and friends could stop in. As noon approached, we'd sit at the ends of our beds, looking down the aisle toward the entrance—hoping to see our own parents or friends walk in. For too many, the visitors didn't appear. I could see their disappointment as they slumped back in their beds.

When kids did see a familiar face, you could hear their screams of joy. I remember that feeling when I saw Mom and Dad walk in. We held each other in long embraces. On nice days, they'd take me outside in my wheelchair for a picnic lunch. On other days, we'd go to a different room to visit. Each visit lasted a couple of hours, and the end was always difficult. I wanted to go home with them. They didn't want to say goodbye and leave me there. In the fall, when the weather deteriorated, on some Sundays they couldn't visit. The moments when I looked down the aisle and didn't see them coming through the door were very sad for me. Usually, in these cases, a nurse came by to let me know they weren't coming that day. That meant I wouldn't see them for two weeks.

My brother and his girlfriend Buzzie, now his fiancée, visited a couple of times, and Aunt Mickey and Cousin Joe surprised me once. On Sundays when my parents couldn't come, I'd usually get a package with comic books, pads of paper, and a nice letter from my mom, who would reassure me that everything would be OK and I'd be "coming home soon."

FIRST LEG

I had my first trip to the prosthetics lab soon after my arrival. There I met a man named Elmer, who managed the lab and oversaw the project of designing and building my leg. Other people were involved, too, through many steps in the process that I really didn't understand. I visited the lab multiple times a week.

The first step was to make a mold of my stump for a new socket (bucket) for my leg. I had to stand between and hold on to two parallel bars while they wrapped Plaster of Paris around the entire stump and around my waist (to hold it in place). I then had to stand on one leg, holding on to parallel bars, for about an hour and wait while the plaster dried. When it was dry, the prosthetics workers cut it away to make a finished mold. This had to be done several times to create a mold that was comfortable and had no pressure points.

The next step was to measure the dimensions of my fully formed left leg and foot—its full length, from hip to knee and knee to foot along with thigh and calf width and foot size. They planned to design the prosthetic leg to conform to my real leg.

My parents had informed the doctors and prosthetics professionals about how physically active I was. Most children being fitted for artificial limbs at the time were trained to walk with either a hip or knee lock mechanism, but not both. My parents felt that having both a hip and a knee lock would allow me to be as active as I'd been before. After many discussions and disagreements, my parents prevailed. These types of locks and their designs were relatively new, and I was sort of a "guinea pig" in having both locks.

With each step in the prosthetics process, I had to test what they'd designed to make sure the leg fit properly and the measurements were correct. The locks they were installing in the leg were new designs, and they needed me to work with the locks to make sure they worked and were easy for me to use. I spent many hours in that lab trying the devices, sitting while they made adjustments, and trying again.

Then I had to learn how to walk with the new leg. It had a totally different "feel" than the peg leg. I had to learn how to walk with a different gait to maintain my balance and coordination. The length of the new leg was longer than my peg leg and very close to the length of my left one. I had to learn how to use the hip and knee locks. They built prototypes so I could work with therapists—unlocking both locks to sit and making sure they were locked when I stood up.

I had to learn how to walk all over again. While the peg leg was extremely light, the new leg was much heavier. I thought it would be easy to master the new one, but the added weight, and the fact that I now had a foot, too, forced me to work harder to step forward and maintain my balance and forward motion. It was a whole new feeling for me, learning how to walk a different way. Hours of practice walking on the prototypes followed, which resulted in more adjustments. There were many days when I felt like I just wanted my peg leg back and I wanted to go home. I feared the new leg would slow me down. Could I run around like I used to? Could I keep up with other kids? The therapists assured me that as I got used to the leg I'd be able to get around and do everything I'd done before. They continually told me this and helped me avoid becoming discouraged.

When my parents had left me off at the hospital in July, my mom had told me I'd be there "for a little while." Mom told me later that she'd expected me to be home after about three months—in time to join my second-grade class. In September, it was apparent my stay at the hospital would be longer. Creating the new leg was progressing very slowly. It wasn't fitting properly, and the length (not accurate) and weight (too heavy) made it hard for me to walk. I was getting frustrated wondering why it was taking so long. I wanted to run and play again. I was tired of either being in a bed, riding in a wheelchair, or trying out the leg. When it was nearly completed, parts of the new leg had to be rebuilt. Mom became very upset at the whole process and the length of time. The prosthetics workers kept making adjustments, which took more time, and their adjustments weren't correcting all the issues.

By September, I knew I wouldn't return home in time to enter second grade. But others had a worse plight: Most of the children at the hospital faced an indefinite stay. Some would be there for years, not months. For that reason, the hospital had its own school, with kindergarten through grade 12. I attended the start of second grade at the hospital, but my memories of that school are very faint. I know that most days I spent a large part of my time either in the lab or with the therapists, not in the classroom.

September came and went. And the months of October and November weren't much different. But I had progressed in walking to the point where the therapists were satisfied. Some issues with the leg still were unresolved as December arrived. The leg was heavy and the locks were cumbersome. Finally, my parents made the decision to bring me home, and on Christmas Eve of 1952, I was released from the hospital.

The "for a little while" Mom had envisioned had turned out to be six months. I was so happy to be home again and simply do the things I'd enjoyed before. I saw smiles on my parents' faces, which I hadn't seen for a while. The best gift that Christmas was being together again at home.

As I look back on that six-month stay at Haverstraw, it was the most difficult time in my life. The nurses, therapists, and prosthetics people were all very kind to me. But for a seven-year-old very active boy, being confined to a bed and a wheelchair, and waiting for a new leg to be finished made it a very dark time in my life. What I did learn was how to cope with being by myself—the silence, the waiting. There was no reason to feel encouraged with all the delays and setbacks. I had no one to talk to. I had to keep my feelings to myself.

More difficult was being separated from my parents. Around them, I always received a word of encouragement, a smile, or a hug. I never felt any anger toward my parents for sending me back to Haverstraw. I knew they loved me–I never had any doubt about that. They made the right decision for me, and it hurt them as much as me to be separated that long. I could see the pain and sadness in their faces. But the goal was a "big picture" one—I needed a new leg to give me better ability to walk and function.

In 2009, in the process of writing my story, I talked to my wife, Kathy, about my time and experience at the hospital in Haverstraw. She asked me if I ever thought about traveling back to visit the hospital where I'd stayed for so many months. Kathy went a step further by emailing the public relations manager about my stays there. She immediately received a response from Mary Creagh, head of public relations, who asked when I was a patient there. With that information, Mary was able to retrieve from the hospital's medical records the admission cards for my stays in 1947 and in 1952. On those cards were descriptions of my condition, my admission dates, and my discharge dates. Mary mailed us copies of those cards. Viewing them, combined with the encouragement of my wife, increased my interest in visiting the hospital again.

In July 2009, my cousin Joe drove Kathy and me to Haverstraw from his home in Syracuse. During the ride, my thoughts returned to my time at the hospital and I must admit I felt a bit anxious. As we passed the exit marked "Monticello," I choked up thinking about my mom and dad and the ride they took many times to the hospital—particularly the trips when they had to drive home without me. I thought, again, about the difficult and emotional decisions they had to make.

When we passed the sign on Route 17 with the words, "Haverstraw— Next Two Exits," it brought back the memory of my second trip to the hospital, sitting in the front seat of the car with my parents and clutching my mom's arm. As we came into town, we could see the entrance to the hospital, now named Helen Hayes Hospital, up on a hill.

As we got out of the car, I was very nervous and really didn't know what to expect. Mary Creagh greeted us and took us on a tour. What happened next surprised me. As we came through a wide door, we entered one of the long, winding, brick-walled hallways I had traveled down many times during my stays. As I walked past each window, I looked out at the back lawn remembering my days sitting in my wheelchair outside. I had an overwhelming feeling I was going to break down and cry. I visualized myself in a wheelchair going to the prosthetics lab or going back to my ward or anywhere else I needed to go.

Mary showed us where my ward was located, now a long row of office cubicles. She showed us the auditorium, where every Friday night all the kids went to watch movies, sitting on gurneys. She showed us the pool where I spent many days in the water. She showed us the outside porch. She took us to a room full of archives and photos chronicling the hospital's history. We found photos from the period I was there, including a photo of the ward where I stayed. Seeing that photo brought back memories of the most difficult days of my life.

Mary took us into the prosthetics lab where I spent many hours. I talked to the manager of the lab about my experience in 1952, and the long process of designing and building my leg. As I talked, he looked back at an older man conversing with one of the lab employees. The man had formerly worked in the lab but was now retired. The manager asked the man, John, to come over and meet me. As I told him about my leg and my hospital stay, he looked at me and said "I must have worked on your leg." I asked him about Elmer, with whom I'd spent most of my time in the lab. "Elmer was my boss," he said. After 57 years, I'd made a connection to my past.

I think back on all those months in the hospital, and realize I got through the experience because of the love and security I always felt from my parents. They knew what had to be done in spite of the pain and tears that came along with it. There were many days when doubts and fear crept into my head, but my trust in my parents helped me endure. My appreciation for what they sacrificed for me is beyond measure.

ANOTHER MOVE, ANOTHER CHALLENGE

The next stage of my life was a blur—coming home from the hospital in December 1952, going back to second grade in Monticello in January, and moving a few weeks later. It was quite a contrast to go from sitting and waiting for six months in the hospital to the hectic pace and many changes of regular life.

In early 1953, my dad earned a management promotion with the phone company, requiring yet another move—this time to Schenectady, New York, which neighbored Albany, the state capital. We moved during the winter, in February, into a new home in a new development in the Schenectady suburb of Niskayuna.

Schenectady was home to one of the largest General Electric (GE) plants in the country, with more than 30,000 employees. The company built a new research and development center in Niskayuna, which brought many new residents to the area. The area economy was growing—new suburbs in the Albany/Schenectady area were developed and new schools were built. The housing development we moved into, which had been a cornfield a year earlier, included only a dozen houses when we moved in, with several others in the distance. Eventually, more than 200 houses were built in our neighborhood. I think we were one of the few non-GE families there.

Our new home was one story, with a full basement. It was a modest home with three bedrooms. Its only bathroom, kitchen, and dining room all were small, but big enough for the three of us. This house had a large living room with a large window in the front. Mom told me they wanted a house with all rooms on one floor to make it easier for me. They also looked for a flat piece of property I could play on. When we moved in, the yard was a combination of snow and mud, as they planned to seed the lawn in the spring. When I looked out my new bedroom window, I saw a flat backyard. I was excited: It would be a great place to run and play.

Soon after we moved in, my mom began meeting other moms in the neighborhood. One of them was Elsie Emery. She had a son, Jimmy, who was a couple of years younger than me, and a daughter, Chris, who was my age. After meeting my mom, and learning about me, she told Jimmy I was handicapped, and encouraged him to meet me. He rang our doorbell one day and I invited him in. I immediately showed him my baseball card collection, and found out he had one, too. We hit it off right away.

During this time, I was getting more comfortable with my new leg. Learning to work the locks, to sit, and then stand up and make sure the locks worked became easier. It was more comfortable with this leg to sit in a chair, on the couch, or in the car, and look like any other sitting person.

I now faced another transition into a new elementary school, Craig School, just a mile from our house. It would be my third school (not counting the school at the hospital) in the space of twelve months. I was entering a second-grade class of kids that had been together since the previous September. Mom told me, again, that I'd be facing a room full of stares at first, and that those stares might continue for several days. It reminded me of the day I walked in the hospital ward for the first time.

Mom prepared the way for me, which I learned later, although I wasn't surprised. She had already talked to the principal and met with some of the teachers. My teacher had talked about me to the kids in my class before I joined them. As I walked in the classroom, and the heads and eyes turned my way, I was very nervous wondering what to expect. But that uneasy feeling disappeared as I was met with smiles from the kids and greeted with a warm handshake from my new teacher. It was a great feeling, and a great start at my new school. The familiar stares happened, but the many smiles made me feel comfortable and accepted from day one.

I had great teachers at that school who always encouraged me, including Mrs. Decker; Mrs. Barker; Mr. Israel; Mr. Torpey, my physical education teacher; and Miss Naylor, my music teacher. I became good friends with Mr. Benny, the school custodian, who came to my aid numerous times when I fell and bent some part in my leg. He'd get a hammer and screwdriver and fix it.

There were times when I was without my artificial leg for a couple of days because it had to be repaired. When that happened, I had to use crutches to get around at school. It made me a little uneasy. On one of those occasions, I decided not to use my crutches and I hopped around the classroom instead. When my classmates and teacher saw me doing it for the first time, I could see them holding their collective breath thinking I was eventually going to fall and hurt myself. My teacher was petrified. But as I hopped and successfully maneuvered, I could see them all beginning to smile. My hopping brought laughter, but in a good way. In fact I remember getting a round of applause sometimes. I think getting my classmates to enjoy my hopping made me feel more comfortable and put them at ease, as well.

The teachers treated me like everyone else, when it came to schoolwork or behavior. My mom warned the teachers: "Don't spoil him! If he needs to be scolded, scold him!" And they did. I simply felt like one of the kids—nobody special—which made me feel accepted the way I was. I received no special treatment. Mom made sure of that.

My favorite teacher was Mrs. Decker, who was both my third- and fourth-grade teacher. We hit if off right away when we found out we both loved baseball. We talked baseball before and after school. She had a son, Johnny, who was a great high-school pitcher and attracted major league scouts. I made my mom take me to some of his games to watch him pitch. Mrs. Decker was there, cheering on her son. She and Mom would cringe and anticipate a fall as I jumped up on the bleachers. But I managed.

Mrs. Decker made those years fun, and she helped me love math by using baseball. To improve my multiplication and division skills, she had me calculate batting averages, win-loss percentages, and earned run averages. When the World Series games played in September, she'd bring a radio into the classroom and allow us to listen while we worked on homework. One year, Mrs. Decker convinced the principal to set up a television in the auditorium, so kids could watch the games right after school. One of those games was memorable—the only no-hit, no-run, perfect game pitched in a World Series by Don Larsen of the New York Yankees in Game 5 of the 1956 series.

Later, for one of her master's degree classes, Mrs. Decker was required to write about a special moment as a teacher. She asked my mom if she could write about me. Here's one excerpt:

> "I well remember the day when Billy came into my room—the broad grin, the rosy cheeks, and the twinkly blue eyes. I must admit the first time he informed me that he was going to go down the slide on the playground, I held my breath and couldn't speak. Billy loved doing challenging things. My class was learning to braid rugs. He was ready for this project too, although I was aware it might not come easily. It was a bit difficult for most of the children to fold the strips of wool with eight fingers and two thumbs. Billy didn't have as many fingers on one hand as the other children. But he made a small mat for his chair.
>
> No doubt, the first and most important thing concerning Billy or any disabled child is that *first* he has to have a *desire* to do things, a *determination* to carry through, and an *optimistic* viewpoint. Billy displays all of these."

My mom and I continued our friendship with Mrs. Decker for many years after that. She and the other teachers at the school were positive influences in my life.

Mrs. Decker (left) with Mom and me

Along with attending a new school, I was still adjusting to walking with my new leg. All my walking that first winter was indoors, due to the snow and ice outside. I also was getting used to sitting differently. I now could unlock my knee and hip and sit more comfortably. Getting up from a chair and remembering to lock the knee and hip before I took a step was a challenge. At the age of seven, I'd always be in a hurry when I got up…forget the locks, and fall to the floor. It happened several times, at home and at school. Mom had the urge to pick me up, but she didn't, and I wouldn't let her, anyway. My teachers would rush to help, but I wanted to get up on my own. My bruises reminded me to slow down.

It wasn't long before spring and warmer weather in our new town. The school had a great playground in back. I couldn't wait to get outside at recess and play on it. I could tell the teachers were watching me, and they were nervous when they saw how active I was. Every day I'd play tetherball with someone. I'd go down the slide sideways with my left leg hitting the slide and my right leg up in the air.

Other kids played kickball. I didn't ask if I could play, I just joined in. I think they were taken aback by my wanting to join in, and by how well I kicked the ball. The other kids began to accept me even more—saying "Hi," talking to me, and being very friendly. Some kids still gawked at me, and I knew that would continue. But my physical differences became secondary to most of the kids. I was feeling really good about myself.

Playing in that playground made me feel more confident running on my new leg, and I began to walk with a better gait. I started running more, and teachers warned me to be careful. Of course, I fell a few times. At first, the other kids ran over to see if I was OK. But after a while, they just expected me to get up. The teachers and the kids eventually felt more at ease—I'd just get up and run again.

The teachers easily could have held me back but, at the urging of my mom, they let me figure things out for myself.

MY NEW LEG MAN

As I became more comfortable with my leg, I was more active with sports and other physical activities. It all put stress on the leg, which sometimes broke some of the parts. Add to that was the fact that I was growing, which made it important to find a prosthetics professional near our home.

The hospital in Haverstraw had referred us to Sunnyview Rehabilitation Hospital in Schenectady—a large, well-respected institution for people with permanent disabilities, impairment from strokes, or other debilitating diseases. The orthopedic staff at Sunnyview wanted to evaluate my condition and see how my leg worked and functioned. The evaluation required me to walk on a stage in front of several doctors and local prosthetic professionals. It was like a beauty pageant, when contestants parade in front of the judges.

The doctors watched me walk back and forth, turn around, and sit on a chair while they talked to each other about my case. Here I was, age eight, walking around on a stage, wearing just my underwear and my leg. It bothered my mom. After about an hour of this, she asked, "Why are you putting him through this?" My condition was very unique because of the amputation at the hip, and because of my high level of physical activity.

After the evaluation at Sunnyview, the doctors and prosthetists referred us to Lyman Dickinson, who owned a prosthetics business in

Watervliet, New York, an old river town about 25 miles from our home. Mr. Dickinson (as I called him) was a man in his 50s who had lost both of his legs in a tragic accident. When he was 20, he'd tried to jump a train and missed. Both legs were caught under the train and both had to be amputated.

Mr. Dickinson was a self-educated man and was very adventurous. He was bright, intelligent, and loved to talk about politics, life, or history. At the age of 70, he bowled a 299 game, which stands as the highest score ever bowled in the nation by a double amputee. He learned the trade of prosthetics at The Hanger Corp., one of the largest prosthetics companies in the world. He eventually opened his own one-man brace shop with occasional help from his brother, Bill.

We began going to him first for leg repairs, and later for new legs. Our visits always lasted much longer than necessary. Mom didn't have the heart to tell to him stop talking, because he was a man with a "heart of gold," she said. Mr. Dickinson charged Mom considerably less than he should have. I needed to have the legs lengthened as I grew, and I needed new ones when I wore them out. Each new leg took about six to seven months to be completed, when it should have taken a month or two. But the end product was always exceptional.

Actually, it was Mr. Dickinson who came up with a very unique hip lock for me, which allowed me to be very active—playing sports, getting around quickly, and not being slowed down. To this day, whenever I show my leg to prosthetic professionals, they're amazed at the design. Mr. Dickinson designed it specifically for me. Any new leg made for me since has incorporated his design.

Mr. Dickinson built a total of three legs for me—all of which stood up to my constant physical activity and pace of life. He was an integral part of my happiness, because he used his skills and knowledge to make a leg that helped me use my capabilities and abilities to the fullest.

Later, when I was in college, one of the legs was taking an especially long time to build. Mom became increasingly upset at him. One Sunday afternoon at school, there was a knock on our fraternity house door and in stepped Mr. Dickinson. In all the years I knew him, he wore the same shirt, same sport coat, and same shoes. But I was so impressed that he drove from Watervliet to our campus in New Jersey (a four-hour trip), to deliver my new leg to me.

He wanted to visit a bit and hear about my new life in college. He took pride in helping me function to the fullest and he felt good about seeing me progress in life. Mr. Dickinson never married, but I think he felt like he had a son in me. Looking back, I remember Mom getting frustrated with him many times. Yet I know she appreciated what he did and the sacrifices he made financially to help us.

Before Mr. Dickinson started making my replacement legs, I would go back to Sunnyview whenever I needed a new one. The appointments usually were with a smaller group of doctors, and invariably their attention would divert to my partial left arm and hand. Because I was born with this condition, I learned to adapt from the beginning. I found that I could grip items between my tiny thumb and the two little fingers that were webbed together. I could hold a cup by bending my arm and cradling it. Most important to me was the ability to grip a baseball bat and a golf club with two hands, and also to fit a baseball glove on my little hand.

The doctors were curious about my hand's functionality. Dr. Bill Gazeley, a prominent orthopedic surgeon in Schenectady, took special interest in me. He talked to my mom many times about my hand. He said something like, "I think I can operate on the left hand and make it more functional, so the thumb could grip things better." I wasn't in favor of it. I convinced the doctors I didn't need the surgery by giving them a grip, and I would almost hurt them with it. I asked, "What would be the advantage?" The only advantage I heard that I liked was that I could catch a baseball, one-handed.

My mom said, "Why? Let's just leave it as it is." I was happy Mom felt that way. I'd already adapted to what I could and couldn't do with the hand. Surgery couldn't give me much more than I already had. It might have allowed me to use tools and unscrew things, but I learned to use them in my own way, anyway.

Most of the stares people directed my way were focused on my hand and arm. Some kids even came up to me to touch it. I found it entertaining to see their reactions. It was almost like they were waiting for my arm to grab them as in a sci-fi movie. My arm and hand looked very different physically than others' did. I had to get used to it.

The biggest hurdle was clothing. Mom had to alter every long-sleeved shirt or coat. Though she knew how to sew, until I came along she'd had no experience shortening to the extent needed for me. She learned how, though, because she had to. I heard the sound of her sewing machine in the house every day. With my level of physical activity, and the resulting rips in clothing, she stayed very busy.

Mom also took me to an occupational therapist at Sunnyview who taught me two other important life skills: how to cut my food safely—with a fork in my left hand and a knife in my right—and how to tie my shoes. The latter took lots of practice, and was a priority because it was embarrassing to ask a teacher to tie them at school.

'LET'S DO IT!'

Aunt Mickey and Mom loved to swim. As teenagers, they swam near their home across the Hudson River and back, several times. Their love for swimming initiated their desire to teach me how to swim.

Aunt Mickey was my greatest encourager when it came to trying physical activities. She was a "Let's do it," "Let's try it," fun-loving person. She and Mom were opposites in some ways, but I needed them both and they complemented each other well. Aunt Mickey helped me develop the confidence to try new things and not worry about failing. She taught me that success comes with trying, and that you only fail if you don't try.

Aunt Mickey (with Uncle Teen)

While Mom was, understandably, fearful and protective, Aunt Mickey said things like, "C'mon, let's let this kid try some things." When we went to visit her, sitting around was *not* an option. She never asked, "Would you like to learn how to swim?" or "Would you like to learn how to play golf?" Instead, she'd say, "We're going to teach you how to swim," or "Let's go and play golf." Her confidence in me helped me build confidence in myself. And it helped my mom realize that the freedom to try physical activities, particularly sports, had a positive effect on my attitude and my happiness.

In her usual way, Aunt Mickey applied her "Let's do it" initiative in introducing me to swimming when I was eight years old, during one of our visits. She took me to a local YMCA and she said, "Billy, I'm going to get you started on learning how to swim." As scared as I was, my aunt wasn't going to take "no" for an answer.

I recall being rather reluctant to even try because I was fearful of failing, or drowning and losing my life. She sensed that. I put my swim trunks on and approached the pool—crutches and all. She instructed me to jump into the water, but I immediately recoiled and chickened out. I did *not* want to jump into the water.

She reassured me that I wasn't going to drown, and I began to reconsider jumping in the water. But she sensed I was still hesitating.

Aunt Mickey promptly put her hands on my waist and *threw* me into the water! Now I was underwater with my eyes closed. It was a very scary moment.

My thought was, "What do I do now?" But the next thing I knew, my aunt was underneath me, helping me float to the surface. She took both my arms and proceeded to teach me how to stroke them through the water, and all the while she stayed beneath me. She told me to kick with my one leg to help me glide.

She was a Red Cross instructor—she knew what she was doing. But I wasn't so sure. Could I swim without her help?

My confidence began to grow, but for a long time I still needed her to hold me up or to hold my body in some way.

After several attempts, she simply let go, and I began to stroke by myself—first, to make sure I didn't drown! I kept thinking I was too young to die! Then I realized I was actually staying on top of the water and stroking my arms on my own, without her help. Aunt Mickey clapped, smiled, and said, "See, I knew you could do it." I was a very happy and proud boy.

From then on, I became a water bug. Whenever I went into the water to swim or play, I'd be in for hours. Whenever we visited during the summer, Aunt Mickey took Joe and me to the pool at the country club or, next door, to the neighbors' small backyard pool.

Also, during many summers, Mom, Aunt Mickey, Cousin Joe, and I rented a cottage on Galway Lake in upstate New York. It was a very still lake, because only rowboats and sailboats were allowed. The cottage we rented had a small beach and a very gradual increase in water depth as you swam away from shore. Joe and I spent many hours playing and swimming. We could go out far from the shore and still not be over our heads. There was a raft about 50 yards from shore, and my aunt taught me how to dive head first off of it.

With my Mom and Dad at Galway Lake

Diving was the kind of challenge I enjoyed—the kind that allowed you to prove to yourself and others that you could achieve something. In my early teens, when friends and I golfed daily at our local country club, we took breaks to head up to the club pool. We played and splashed more than we swam.

In the pool with Jimmy Emery (left) and his sister, Chris (middle)

Enjoying a break at the pool one day, I began to watch other kids dive off the low- and high-diving boards. It looked like so much fun, and I had the urge to try it. Usually, I'd ask my mom first about trying a new physical activity. In this case, she wasn't there, so I just did it. I mentioned the idea to my friend, Jimmy Emery, who went up to tell one of the lifeguards about my idea. The lifeguard and Jimmy came back and talked to me, and I convinced them I could do it.

I had my heart set on the high board which came as a surprise to them. With my crutches, I walked over to the high-dive ladder. I then realized how high it was! I dropped my crutches and maneuvered up one step at a time, my one leg pushing me up to the next step and my stump resting on each step. It seemed like it took forever to get to the top. In the meantime, kids and parents began noticing me—and most of the kids were laughing. My friends, including Jimmy, cheered me on.

As I reached the board, I looked down, saw the height, and nearly chickened out. I decided not to look down again.

My heart was pounding and I had to catch my breath. I focused my eyes on the board, took short hops to the end, stopped, and quickly jumped feet first.

All I remember next was hitting the water and rushing to the surface. I was met with mostly kids' laughter—but also applause! My friends went crazy. I'd attempted something new, and succeeded at it. (My mom wasn't thrilled when she came to the pool and heard about it. I think she tried to hide a smile, though.)

Many children—those with disabilities and others—were prevented from trying this type of activity for fear of something bad happening. My mom and my aunt could have sheltered me from learning how to swim or kept me away from the water just to protect me, or even to give them peace of mind. Instead, they exposed me to a new experience, a fun thing to do, an activity that continued to build my self-confidence. It also led to a lifelong love for being in the water.

Their confidence in me (and my own confidence) grew as I showed the ability to do more physical activities, and to handle them safely. I realized if I really wanted to do something, I shouldn't be afraid to try.

THE IMPACT OF SPORTS

The pursuit of sports has always been a very positive force in my life. Many of my earliest memories include the joy of going to the backyard and playing ball or running. I always had so much energy and early encounters with sports are some of the happiest times in my life. As I grew old enough to play team sports, I was usually the organizer of baseball, basketball, or football games in someone's backyard.

Our house in Schenectady had a level, rectangular backyard. Instead of viewing it as a yard of green grass, I thought of it as a playing field.

One spring after all the snow had melted, my friend Jimmy Emery came over to visit. He saw a baseball mitt in my bedroom and we decided to go outside and play catch. I'm not sure if Jimmy knew what to expect. Was he thinking: Can this kid really catch a ball with his little hand and throw it? Can he run after a ball?

Since I had no way to grip the ball with my left hand, I learned to catch it by guiding the ball into my mitt and covering and securing it with my right hand. Jimmy started off lobbing the ball to me, not sure if I could catch it. This caused some awful throws from him that rolled away from me. He found out right away, though, that I could run to retrieve an errant throw. After several throws, I began throwing the ball back harder and straighter to him, which surprised him. We continued to make longer throws to each other until we were exhausted. That was the beginning of a long and close friendship. I consider Jimmy my best childhood friend.

Jimmy loved to play all sports like I did, and we joined other neighborhood kids who shared our passion. Depending on the season, we organized games in several backyards, particularly mine and Jimmy's. His family's property had a very large, level backyard that was the perfect shape for a baseball field and could also be used as a larger football field. Some neighborhood kids were regulars (Jackie Lauroesch, Joe Flora, Billy Hunt, Pete Johnson, Terry Clark, Joe Skelton, Jimmy, and me), and others played from time to time. The "regulars" telephoned each other or arranged certain times, during summer days or after school, when we'd all meet at someone's backyard.

In the summer, we'd play all day—taking a quick break to go home for lunch and then spending the rest of the day playing games together. All the moms knew where we were from the yelling and talking that reverberated through the neighborhood. We probably had a total of 10-12 kids in that group—all within about a three- or four-year age span. It was a great group, and we all got along with each other.

We were very competitive, though. We all wanted to win. I was one of the more competitive kids, with an intense desire to win. Sometimes, we got so mad at each other that the fists came out and we all headed home. But invariably we'd be back playing together in a couple of hours.

Probably the most popular game we played was baseball. Initially, we played with a tennis ball at the request of my mom, who saw many windows in the vicinity. Around that time, the wiffle ball was introduced, which turned out to be the greatest invention ever made for us. It was a perforated plastic ball with holes in it that allowed you to throw fast, throw curve balls, and (if you were angry at someone) throw balls at opponents' bodies without hurting them. We used a plastic bat and we didn't need gloves. We generally didn't throw very fast—otherwise, we'd never hit the ball.

Because our backyards were the perfect sizes and shapes for sports, even younger kids and girls joined in the activities. We chose teams before every game, which was quite a ritual. Jimmy and I usually were the captains and chose sides. We'd play for hours. Even as we got older and bigger, we always enjoyed a wiffle ball game every so often.

As we grew, we started playing baseball on a larger field at an open corner lot, behind a church—just down the street from my house. We started using a regulation hardball and wooden bats, and we fielded balls with baseball gloves. One of my greatest memories during those years came when Mom told me my birthday present was a new, regular-size baseball glove. I'd always dreamed about having a regulation-size baseball mitt like the major leaguers had. I'd had gloves before, but they were designed for small kids.

Mom took me to an Army/Navy store to pick out a glove. My heart was pounding and my excitement was off the charts. My hand was very small but I found a glove that fit well enough that I could keep it on my hand. It was a Nellie Fox second-baseman mitt. The smell of the new leather glove was wonderful—like the smell of the interior of a new car. I immediately ran over to Jimmy's house to show it to him. My dad showed me how to make the glove more flexible, and how to form a pocket by rubbing oil in the palm of the mitt and putting a tight rubber band around it when I wasn't using it. I even slept with that glove for a few days. It was my prized possession.

During the school year, in the fall and spring, we'd meet up after dinner and play football, basketball, or baseball until it was too dark, or when our parents told us to get home to do our homework. As we got older, football turned into tackle football without pads, which led to occasional fights and kids coming to tears. But everybody always came back to play again later.

When we had to play inside, my basement was a popular hangout because of our collection of games. Dad and my brother loved to play ping-pong, and dad built a plywood regulation table long before I was born. My parents also found a used pool table that was smaller than regulation size, but was a great size for kids. I learned how to cradle the pool cue on top of my small left hand. Dad also hung a basketball net on one wall, and when we played inside we used a rubber ball. We formed leagues for each game and it became very competitive.

For Christmas one year, I had asked for a table hockey game I'd seen in a local toy store a few months earlier. By turning a knob attached to each player, you could move a player's hockey stick to swipe at a small blue marble, which served as a puck. The game had a handle behind each goalie, allowing you to move him left or right to block the marble.

On Christmas Day, I had opened every present except one. The remaining present had the shape of this game. I opened it, anticipating this would be it. Although it was a table hockey game, it was a different one. I tried to look happy, but my heart sank. I tried to look excited and I began playing it so I wouldn't hurt my parents' feelings.

As we were cleaning up all the wrapping paper, Mom went over to our couch and reached behind it to retrieve a brown package. She said they had one extra gift for me. I was still glum over not getting the hockey game I'd wanted, but I was curious. As I opened the package, and peeled away the brown paper, I saw what it was – the hockey game I'd asked for!

I was so excited, I couldn't say anything…I didn't know what to say. As I looked at my parents, they both started laughing and I let out a scream of joy—what a great surprise. Mom told me afterward that she had ordered the game I wanted from FAO Schwarz, the children's toy store in New York City. It hadn't arrived by two days before Christmas so she went out and bought the other one so I wouldn't be totally disappointed. On Christmas Eve, in the afternoon, an American Express delivery truck drove into our driveway with the brown package. Mom decided to make it a surprise and hid it behind the couch. That game was my all-time favorite, and we played it for many years.

At some point, my buddies became interested in bowling. Our parents took turns driving us to local bowling alleys on Saturdays. My dad and brother were good bowlers, and I enjoyed watching them when I was little. I learned the game by watching them. Mom found a used, lighter-weight bowling ball that I could handle. It was just another sport that I picked up quickly and enjoyed.

Sports, the highlights of my childhood, built up my self-confidence because I could compete effectively with my friends. I surprised them with my abilities and competitiveness. We all learned how to get along whether we won or lost.

I learned from playing these games that I was naturally competitive and had a strong desire to win and succeed. All the other guys were fierce competitors, too. There was never a time when we'd back off or slow down, particularly when we played against each other. That competitive fire, for the most part, has been a great asset for me, although there were times when it was excessive.

One time, in the middle of a baseball game in my backyard, during a play I slid into second base. In our games, we had no umpire, so the team in the field also made the "out" or "safe" calls for each play on base. On this particular play, I slid into base and thought I was safe. The other team called me "Out!" I immediately got up and started yelling, including a very loud profanity, which my mother heard from inside the house.

In front of all of my friends, Mom marched into the middle of the backyard, grabbed me by the shoulder, and marched me back into the house. The other kids disappeared very quickly. A stern lecture followed. I learned I had "crossed the line."

Even though my friends thought it was funny, my mom had a different opinion. Very rarely did I see her that upset. Because of my respect for her, I realized my actions were probably as bad as they sounded. It was one of those defining moments in your life that cause you to change. It wasn't the last time I lost my temper, but those instances became few and far between.

Throughout this entire time period, what I appreciated most about my parents was that they allowed me to play all these games in spite of the wear and tear on my prosthetic leg, the numerous breakages caused by all the physical activity, and the cost of repairing and replacing the leg (not to mention a couple of fingers and other body parts I managed to break). It would have been very logical and understandable for them to tell me, "You can't play anymore because you're continually breaking your leg."

One moment, in particular, touched me deeply. During a baseball game at the corner lot, my knee lock came loose and I couldn't put weight on that leg without falling. My friends helped me home. Mom opened the front door, shook her head, and said, "Get in the car. We'll go over to Mr. Dickinson's shop."

We drove there, got the leg repaired, and returned home later the same day. I called my friends and we started up a new game. About 30 minutes into this new game, I decided to slide into a base to beat a throw. When I got up, it felt like my right leg was a lot shorter. I looked down and saw that my right foot had broken apart from the leg. My friends helped me home again.

Mom saw me coming and was already in the car, ready to take me back to Mr. Dickinson. As I got in the car, I looked over at Mom. She had burst out in uncontrollable tears. The weight and responsibility of being my mom and caregiver had hit a breaking point. I felt awful—realizing at that moment the weight of the burden she took on for me. I just sat there, silent, feeling bad for her and guilty for what I had done.

I said to Mom, "I'll never play baseball again, I promise you. I'm sorry." At that point, with her tears still flowing, she looked me in the eye and said, "Don't say that. I don't want you to feel that way." That was my mom, taking the brunt of it, but encouraging me even during times like these that were very stressful for her.

I'm sure during private moments my mom prayed and cried many times, but she never stopped me from playing. My parents knew how much playing sports meant to me, and what an impact it had on my confidence and relationships with other kids. It was the greatest gift my parents could give me, and a big sacrifice on their part.

DREAMING

It was a beautiful Saturday afternoon. The sun was shining on the field, and there was a capacity crowd at Yankee Stadium in New York City. The crowd was buzzing because, in the top of the ninth inning, my team, the New York Yankees, was playing the Boston Red Sox, our fiercest rival. The game was tied 1-1. The Red Sox had runners on second and third, two outs, and their best hitter was up to bat. One more out and we'd get a chance to win the game when we got to bat.

Our pitcher wound up and threw a fast ball. The batter, their best hitter, promptly hit it to deep, left center field. Here I was, playing center field for the Yankees, and I had to catch the ball or the Sox would go ahead. I thought of my hero, Mickey Mantle, who played center field and was considered one of the greatest players ever to wear a Yankee uniform. I needed to run as fast as Mickey and catch up with this ball.

I ran and ran and ran as hard as I could. I caught sight of the ball, reached out as far as I could with my glove, and caught it…just before I ran into the outfield wall. The crowd roared, and I ran in from the outfield to the dugout and was mobbed by my teammates.

It was now the bottom of the ninth, and we were up at bat. I was the first batter up. I faced Boston's best pitcher, and all I wanted to do was make contact with the ball, get a hit, and get on base. We only needed one run to win. I usually took the first pitch and didn't swing, and the pitcher knew my tendencies. He decided to throw a fast ball right down the middle, thinking I wouldn't swing, and get a first strike. But something came over me and I just couldn't resist. The pitch was right down the middle, and right in the zone I liked. I swung as hard as I could and the pitch met the sweet part of the bat. It took off high and deep toward left field. I ran as hard as I could to first base, and as I rounded first, a roar started.

I heard it from the dugout: "Home run! Home run! We won! We won!" I ran around the bases, feeling an exhilarating chill up my spine, and was met at home plate by all my teammates. They jumped all over me as I stepped onto home plate. We'd beaten the hated Red Sox in the bottom of the ninth! What a thrill! I was the hero for the day! I had met my dream of winning a game for the New York Yankees with a home run. It was the greatest feeling of my life. I'd reached the pinnacle—centerfielder and hero for the New York Yankees!

Suddenly, there was a tap...several taps, on my shoulder. "Bill, it's time for dinner."

Unfortunately, I woke up and realized I was not at Yankee Stadium. I was home in my bed taking a nap. But the dream certainly was worth it. I kept closing my eyes to see my home run again, and I was out of breath from excitement.

One of my childhood dreams was to be a baseball player, and especially to play for the Yankees—my favorite team (and Dad's). I wanted to play center field like my hero, Mickey Mantle. I played many imaginary games in my backyard by myself, trying to imitate Mickey's swing, mimicking how he caught the ball and ran the bases, and imagining playing in Yankee Stadium. Just visualizing it was a thrill. I must admit, as I grew older I had many similar dreams of standing in center field—running after and catching fly balls.

Every year, my dad took me to a Sunday afternoon game at Yankee Stadium, usually to watch a double-header. It was a 2 ½-hour drive from Schenectady down to New York City. Back in the 1950s, major league teams usually played two games on a Sunday—a popular day to take kids because the games were in the afternoon. Before we got there Dad would say, "We'll stay for all of the first game and half of the second game, and then we'll head home."

Every year, we sat in a different place at the Stadium, and every year my biggest thrill was watching Mickey Mantle come to bat or tracking down fly balls with his speed in center field. He wore No. 7, which has always been my favorite number.

He was my hero in part because, as a child, he was diagnosed with chronic osteomyelitis, a degenerative condition that caused inflammation of bone, which affected his ankles and legs. Mickey Mantle was passionate about baseball and he played through the pain. In spite of his condition, he was the fastest base-runner in all of baseball, and he got many hits from bunting and beating out throws to first base.

Seeing Mickey Mantle play, with a bad leg, left no doubt in my mind that I would play baseball in Little League and in high school. I knew I was good enough to make a team. I thought I could run fast enough to play and show the coach that I could hit the ball consistently. Teams always needed good hitters. I was confident I would make a team because I was as good as my friends. They had seen firsthand how well I played, how well I hit the ball, and how much I loved to play baseball.

I would have been sadly disappointed in myself if I didn't try. That desire to try—and to actually be able to do activities, like playing baseball—kept me going.

LITTLE LEAGUE TRY-OUT

In the spring of 1954, shortly before I turned nine, I decided to try out for the Niskayuna Little League (the local league). I'd heard about Little League the year before, when my father took me up to the Little League field to watch a game.

In 1953, the Schenectady Little League all-star team brought a lot of excitement to the area by advancing all the way to the championship game at the Little League World Series in Williamsport, Pennsylvania (They lost and were runner-ups). Their series games were broadcast over the radio, and listening to the games increased my interest even more. Many of my friends were going to try out or were already playing Little League.

Playing in our neighborhood games with all of them, I knew I could hit and field as well, or better, than they could. I knew I couldn't run as fast, but I could run. And I thought surely I'd be good enough to make a team. My parents were very hesitant, probably because they didn't want me to be disappointed. Also, as any parent would be, they were concerned that I would hurt myself. But I insisted that I wanted to try, and as always, they didn't get in the way of me making an attempt.

On the short drive to the tryouts, Mom and Dad told me, "Now don't expect to get picked. Just try, but don't be disappointed if you don't make it. It'll be okay." They were expecting I might be disappointed. They wished me luck, though, as I ran over to join the group of kids waiting to try out. I didn't know most of the kids, since they came from other neighborhoods. Although it wasn't unexpected, many of them stared at my left arm, and I'm sure they wondered why I was even trying out.

I clearly remember the first round of tryouts. It had been a beautiful sunny day, and the tryouts were held in the evening, so parents could attend and fill out the applications. The Little League field was just a mile from our home, and was located on the junior high-school grounds. The field had beautiful green grass in the outfield and infield, a smooth dirt infield, and names of local businesses painted on the outfield fences.

I was so excited and couldn't wait to bat and get on the field. There was a long line of boys, organized by age, waiting to get up to bat for evaluation of our batting skills. I watched each boy in front of me make contact with about half the balls pitched to them. I said to myself, "I can do better than they can." Eventually, it was my turn and I could see my parents watching nervously. I noticed a lot of the kids stopped what they were doing and looked my way—curious about what would happen when I came to bat.

The coach on the pitching mound was a little hesitant when he saw me. I think he was a bit surprised seeing me walk up to the plate with a stiff right leg and a short left arm. I imagine he was thinking things like, "Should I lob the ball in? Will it be safe for him to play?"

I immediately got up to bat, into my batting stance, and was ready for the pitch. I had figured out a way, from all my playing, to grip the bat with both hands, swing through the ball, and make contact. I was very nervous, but confident. The first few pitches he threw were soft tosses and way off the plate. I soon yelled out to him, politely saying, "It's okay to throw hard to me."

He started throwing harder and I hit every ball thrown to me into the outfield, some on the ground, some in the air, but all hit squarely. I could see the surprised look on the coach's face. I felt giddy after completing my turn.

I got in a line to field ground balls in the infield and throw over to first base. I had to improvise on how I wore a baseball glove on my small left hand. I had to learn to tuck two of my tiny fingers into one finger slot and my small thumb into another. I couldn't make a grip, but I learned to cover the baseball as it hit the pocket of the mitt. I fielded several ground balls successfully and threw accurately over to first. I did have a little trouble moving to my right due to my leg. But I felt good about my effort and definitely felt like I had done as well as anyone else.

One of the coaches then sent me into the outfield to catch fly balls. It was almost like they were trying to hit fly balls they knew I couldn't catch, but I caught most of them. To their surprise and mine, I caught at least a dozen fly balls without a problem, despite looking up at a bright sun. I ran off the field after all the required drills and felt like saying "I made it! I made it!"

More than a hundred kids tried out, and I felt I had proved myself among the best of them. After the tryouts, my friend Jimmy told me how he couldn't believe how well I hit the ball. I went home that night and couldn't sleep, looking forward to the next day when we'd be told whether we made a team or not. There was no doubt in my mind that I would be on one of the teams. I was looking forward to wearing a baseball uniform and being a member of a team.

All the kids arrived at the field the next day to find out if they'd made the cut. Mr. Kessler, one of the league's leaders and a coach, saw Mom and me, and walked toward us. His son, Steve, had hit many home runs the year before and was considered the best player in the league. He had been one of the coaches who observed me during tryouts.

I was so excited to hear about what team I made. I knew from talking to all my friends that I clearly had performed better than most kids during tryouts.

Unfortunately, the news wasn't what I expected.

Mr. Kessler looked at Mom, and then he looked sadly down at me and said, "Billy, I'm sorry, but we can't let you play in the Little League, because we're afraid you're going to either hurt yourself or somebody else because of your artificial limb." Coach Kessler was afraid if I slid into someone I would injure them, or I would break my leg. Back then, the worry wasn't about liability...it was about safety.

I was devastated. I wanted to go home right away. I wanted to cry. I went from exhilaration and excitement to feeling like I'd been kicked in the stomach. Why the worry about hurting someone or getting hurt? I'd played baseball and football with other kids for hours and nobody had been hurt. I saw the possibility that my sports involvement could come to an end, even though I was as good as or better than many of the other kids.

The most important thing in my life was being taken away.

But I held it in. I wanted to yell at the coach. In my mind, what he'd decided was unfair. He was taking away my chance to play baseball—my favorite sport. I couldn't imagine standing outside the fence, watching other kids who weren't as good as me playing on a team. I'd gone to the field that night excited about joining a team and playing baseball on a beautiful baseball field and now that opportunity was taken away.

Before I could say anything or bolt away, he gently took my arm, bent down next to me, and looked me in the eye. I could tell from the expression on his face that breaking the news to me was very difficult for him. He then said with a smile, "I have an idea for you. My team needs a bat boy. You would be responsible for getting the bat ready for the next batter, picking it up after they hit, and being an encourager on the bench. And, you'd get a uniform."

As sad and heartbroken as I was, I was half listening—not knowing how to feel. The coach put his arm on my shoulder and I began to feel better about it. I don't know what came over me, but I immediately yelled out, "Yes!" His team wore grey uniforms with red trim, and the town fire department sponsored the team. It would be a thrill to get a uniform and a number. His was the favored team, with his 12-year-old son, Steve, back for his last year. That was the start of me being directly involved as part of a team sport. Actually, it turned out to be a great experience—being and feeling part of a team, even though my burning desire to play on the field raged inside of me.

Looking back, I don't know what made me say "yes" right away. It just came out of my mouth without me thinking. I wanted to be part of a baseball team. Although I couldn't play, the role of team batboy gave me the chance to fulfill that desire. In retrospect, I have to believe God made me say, "Yes, I'll do it." The only other option was walking away feeling sorry for myself. Surely it was an immediate reaction. My parents were thrilled, probably because they knew I wouldn't get hurt. They also saw my reaction of being involved in Little League, along with my friends.

Immediately after hearing from Coach Kessler about my new role as bat boy, another league official, accompanied by another man, approached us and said, "There's someone here who would like to meet you." That person was Al DeSantis, the sports editor for the city's main newspaper, *The Schenectady Union-Star.* He had been at tryouts to support his son, Warren, and had seen me go through the hitting and fielding tryouts. After we were introduced, he told me how impressed he was by my courage and attitude, and asked if he could write a story about me for the newspaper!

My mom was very hesitant, and I think it was more out of protection than anything else. I think she was worried about sensationalizing my situation or making a big deal about it. She wasn't ashamed, just being a protective mom. But Al soon won my mom over, and we made an appointment for him to come to our house later that week.

When Al arrived, he brought along a news photographer. We sat on the front porch for a long time and he asked me a lot of questions about my love for the game of baseball. I told him how much I wanted to play baseball—that it was difficult for me to accept the fact that I couldn't play. He explained to me that the story would be about my desire and courage to try out for Little League, and that it might inspire people when they read about me. We also talked about sports in general. More than an hour passed. That conversation was the start of a long friendship between us.

The news photographer began throwing me baseballs, had me field ground balls in our front yard, and asked me to pose for them. He took photos of me in my batting and fielding stances. It was all very exciting. Al was polite enough to call my mom a few days later and tell her what he had written, which really put her at ease.

My batting stance

My fielding stance

The article came out on May 18, 1954, and, to our surprise, the story and my picture were on the front page! The headline read, "Billy Schultz, 8, Bids for Little League Berth, You Spell It C-O-U-R-A-G-E." Mom and dad received several phone calls from friends and also people in the neighborhood, including many they had never met. The next day in school, I got a lot of smiles and pats on the back from my classmates and teachers. Mom called someone she knew at the Kingston newspaper, the Daily Freeman, which ran the same article the next day. (My parents still had many friends there.) The story was picked up by several newspapers around the country.

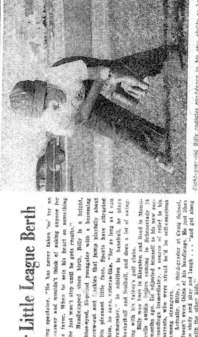

Weather
Fair and Cool

SCHENECTADY UNION-STAR

City
Edition

Now in Its 99th Year of Service in the Public Interest

FULL ASSOCIATED PRESS AND UNITED PRESS SERVICE

VOL. XLIII, NO. 158   SCHENECTADY, N.Y., TUESDAY, MAY 18, 1954   PRICE, FIVE CENTS

PHONE 4-3131

You Spell It C-O-U-R-A-G-E

Billy Schultz, 8, Bids for Little League Berth

By AL DeSANTIS

The application said he loved baseball and wanted to play, and that if he couldn't make the grade as a player he hoped to be a manager or batboy.

There was a line, perhaps added as an afterthought, that he was handicapped.

Niskayuna Little League officials looked over the card in the press box, then stepped out on the field for a look at the young applicant who was trying out for a place in the league with some 150 other small-fry.

What they saw was a terrible bundle of courage —a boy with an artificial leg and half an arm. 8-year-old Billy Schultz of 2022 Fairlawn Parkway. He hobbled after grounders, caught tosses close with the gloved hand of his short left arm, but did as well as the other 8-year-olds. In his enthusiasm could be detected the determination he wouldn't step aside for anyone and the confidence he would be among the 18 in his age group who would be picked for league play this year.

"He has always been SO determined," said his mother, Mrs. Addison A. Schultz, an admir-

ing spectator. "He has never taken 'no' for an answer and wouldn't think of asking anyone for a favor. When he sets his heart on something he just won't stop until he gets results."

Handicapped since birth, Billy is a bright, blue-eyed, 55-pound youngster with a beaming crew-cut and freckles that jump playfully about his pleasant little face. Sports have attracted him, he says, veteran-like, "for as long as I can remember," in addition to baseball, he plays basketball and football, and does a lot of swinging with his father's golf clubs.

Billy was born in Kingston and lived in Monticello awhile before coming to Schenectady 18 months ago. He adjusted himself to his new surroundings immediately, a source of relief to his parents, who were afraid he'd be self-conscious among strangers.

Actually, Billy, a third-grader at Craig School, doesn't even think of his handicaps. He just likes to study and play and laugh . . . "and get along with the other kids."

The odds are against Billy Schultz making the Little League, but at 8 he's already a backstopper.

Billy Schultz, son of Mr. and Mrs. Addison A. Schultz, 2022 Fairlawn, Niskayuna, has that determined look in his eyes as he gets ready to climb one more the fence during tryouts for berth assignments in the Niskayuna Little League.

Eight-year-old Billy radiates confidence in his own ability as he stoops to field a grounder besetting his way. Handicaps? Young Mr. Courage doesn't know the meaning of the word.

Front-page newspaper article (May 1954)

The article was well-done, and my parents felt proud. It also encouraged me—to have someone write about my desire and ability to play a game like baseball and other sports, despite my limitations. I had never expected that recognition.

Any recognition I'd received in the past had been from people I'd known—my parents, friends, and aunt and uncle. But having the sports editor of the city's newspaper write a front-page story about me was very uplifting.

The writer, Al DeSantis, and I kept in regular touch over the years, seeing each other at local baseball games, talking over the phone, and later when I was in high school where his son, Warren, was my good friend and a star player on the basketball team. As I progressed through junior high, high school, and college, Al wrote follow-up articles about my accomplishments in sports and in life. In the year he retired, he wrote a letter to my parents, and called my story, "the most inspirational story he had written during his entire career."

No Greater Inspiration in Schenectady Sports

Billy Schultz Plays Them All With One Leg, Withered Arm

By AL DeSANTIS ★★★★★★★
Sports Editor
★★★★★★★

TIME OUT

★★★★★★★★★★★★★★★★★

BASEBALL, BASKETBALL, football, golf, tennis, swimming, bowling.

Thirteen-year-old Billy Schultz tries them all . . . with one leg and a withered left arm.

Schenectady sports has no greater inspiration than this sunny-dispositioned, befreckled, fast-growing 5 foot 8 son of a New York Telephone construction supervisor.

It would be so easy to curl up and watch the parade go by, but Billy Schultz, born handicapped, wants to squeeze everything out of the he-man's sports world his physical limitations permit.

He asks no quarter.

"Be as rough with me as you would anyone else," he begs opponents.

And when he goes down, he bounces up, ready for anyone or anything.

I've traveled far and wide and taken in the great sports events of the country. The World Series, the thunderous bouts of Joe Louis and Rocky Marciano, the golf tournaments embracing Ben Hogan and Sam Snead and Cary Middlecoff, to name some.

But my most stirring moment came at a Little League park . . . Niskayuna's . . . five years ago, produced by then-8 Billy Schultz. Standing on one leg and with his crippled arm, he was trying to beat out boys up to 12 years old for places on the team. It was an indescribable thrill watching the bundle of courage giving the odds the wink.

When he can't make the team, Billy invariably winds up in the "office," like his current position as varsity basketball manager at Van Antwerp Junior High, and

league scorer, as he was for the Niskayuna Babe Ruth League last summer. Statistics fascinate him. He keeps records of the major leagues, the National Football League, the National Basketball Association.

The youngster is an excellent swimmer, has had a nine-hole golf score in the low 60's and has bowled a high game of 160. He is a bright eighth-grade student at Van Antwerp, plays the trumpet, sings bass in the school choir and is a good church boy.

His parents, Mr. and Mrs. Addison Schultz, 2023 Fairlawn Parkway, are continually moved by Billy's dexterity, courage and general outlook on life.

"That boy is a daily inspiration in our lives," they say, humbly. "He has made us the proudest parents on earth." . . .

BUNDLE OF COURAGE—That's Billy Schultz, shown bowling and in church.

Article written during my junior high years (1958)

18 Schenectady UNION-STAR, Tuesday, June 6, 1967

Courageous Billy Schultz Makes It Big At Rutgers

Recalled as One-Armed, One-Legged 8-Year-Old Candidate for 1954 Niskayuna LL

Al DeSantis
Sports Editor

IT WAS TRYOUT TIME for the Niskayuna Little League this warm May night in 1954.

The skinny-armed kids were whistling the ball across the plate, the bigger ones were shooting for the fence.

And an 8-year-old kept getting up and falling down.

That was my first look at Billy Schultz—and the most inspiring moment of my journalistic career.

He was trying to win a Little League berth with one arm and one leg.

He didn't have a chance, of course. Courage could only take him so far. But I made a note to watch him.

"This kid has guts," I remarked. "This kid has guts. He may miss as an athlete, but not in life."

Well, here we are, June 1967, and William Addison Schultz, 21, five-eleven, 173, is holding a B.S. degree awarded him recently at Rutgers University and waiting to start on the GE financial management training program here June 26.

He was quite the young man down there in New Brunswick, N.J. To wit: "B" student . . . manager of the varsity lacrosse team as a sophomore . . . member of the freshman golf team . . . president of the junior honorary society . . . treasurer of his fraternity . . . member of the Glee Club and Choir which gave 75 performances within 24 days in Holland, Switzerland, France, Germany and Austria last year . . . chairman of the campus' record-breaking Community Chest drive in his junior year . . . the star of "Billy Schultz' Sports Show" once a week for four years over the campus radio station . . . the play-by-play broadcaster of Rutgers' baseball and basketball games three years.

It all added up to inclusion in "Who's Who in American Universities."

Billy sprung to Rutgers from Niskayuna High, where he managed football, basketball and baseball teams four years.

He's happy things have broken so well for him "only because my good luck may inspire other handicapped persons."

He had a rewarding summer last year when he worked with mentally retarded children at Saranac Lake.

"If I ever tire of business, I'm going to help kids like that," Billy says. "They can tee all the help and all the friends they can get."

Billy is one of two sons of Mr. and Mrs. Addison Schultz, Fairlawn Parkway. His father is a construction supervisor for New York Telephone. His brother, Richard, 34, a graduate of St. Lawrence, is an engineer for the same company in Poughkeepsie.

As a hard working man, he just bought his father's car. "That gave me a break on it," he smiles. "The price was right."

Dad Schultz is so proud of his courageous son he would have given him a showroom. . . .

Billy Schultz
. . . the word is courage

Article written after my graduation from college (June 1967)

In 2009, as I was thinking about writing my own story, Warren, his son, called me. We hadn't spoken for more than 30 years. He called to tell me his father had passed away, and that when he was going through his dad's old file, he came across a copy of that newspaper published in May of 1954 that had my article on the front page. His dad had spoken many times about the impact of my story on him, personally, and he wasn't surprised his dad had kept a copy. Warren sent me a laminated copy of the front-page article which I now have framed in my office.

But those articles were more than just recognition of my achievements.

They were a tribute to my parents—confirming that their support and encouragement made all the difference in the world. They easily could have held me back from tryouts, and said, "It would be too dangerous," or "You're not good enough to make it." Instead, they let me try and, in my opinion, they let me succeed. It was one of many instances in which my parents allowed me to try something not knowing what the results would be.

That first year of my Little League experience, the Niskayuna Little League all-star team advanced through the regional tournament with ease. It was a team with many gifted players, some of whom later played minor league baseball. We'd been an unknown team, since our league had just started up a couple of years before. We ran up against the largest league in the area—the Schenectady Little League. Their all-star team, which had advanced to the Little League World Series championship game the year before (they lost), also had swept through three easy wins. The winner of our game would go to the state, and then the regional, tournament. And the winner of that tournament would advance to the Little League World Series in Williamsport, Pa.

I was named the bat boy for the all-star team that year, which was a true honor. I think the coaches recognized my enthusiasm for the game and rewarded me for it. The game was held at their park and attracted a huge crowd, with people filling the seats and standing along the outfield fences. Schenectady Little League was heavily favored, with most of its World Series team back from the previous year.

The game was very exciting, with each team trading the lead. In the top of the sixth and final inning, with our team behind 6-5, our best hitter, Gene Galusha, hit a two-run home run to put us ahead 7-6. Our bench went nuts. In my excitement, I ran toward home plate to pick up the bat and to wait for and shake hands with our hero as he crossed home plate, a usual ritual for a batboy. Our next batter, Steve Kessler (Coach Kessler's son) was on deck.

As he prepared to go to bat, he took one last swing in the on-deck circle. As I ran by him to get to home plate his bat hit me square on my left jaw. The force of the bat knocked me immediately to the ground. I stayed conscious, but the next thing I remember clearly was being in the dugout with ice on my jaw and the sensation that my teeth were crooked.

My mom and dad came to the side of the dugout. Mom thought I had been hurt seriously but the coaches calmed her down. A couple of players lifted me over the fence and my dad carried me to the car. I didn't want to leave the game, but Coach Kessler gave me no choice. My parents drove me to the local hospital, where I was diagnosed with a broken left jaw and a dislocated right jaw. Dr. Hamm, our family dentist for many years, willingly came to the hospital late that night and spent two hours cleaning out my mouth and affixing rubber bands to hold my jaw shut. For the next six weeks, I lived on Gerber baby food. It was the only kind of food I could sip.

(By the way, the Schenectady Little League came back to win that game, and two weeks later returned to Williamsport to become Little League World Series champs.)

Two good things happened from all this: The next morning, I looked out our front window and saw several cars driving up and parking in front of our house. Out of the cars stepped the entire Niskayuna Little League all-star team, led by Steve and his dad.

When Mom opened the door, Steve started crying and said, "Mrs. Schultz, I'm so sorry, and I brought something for Billy. I've brought my entire comic book collection. It's in my car, and I want Billy to have it." The collection included more than 500 comic books. My mom hugged

Steve, telling him she was so appreciative of his thought, but that his comic book collection should remain his.

The whole team came in for a few hours. Steve looked sad but cheered up when he saw me smiling. Mom made lunch and lemonade. It was a wonderful feeling to have the entire team at the house to show their concern for me. Here it was, less than a day after they'd lost a crucial game—the most important game in their lives up to that point—and they were at my house! It was a great example of what the word "team" meant. We were in it together.

Two weeks later, after the Schenectady team had won the Little League World Series, there was another knock on our door. The man at the door was Mike Maietta, the head coach of the Schenectady Little League All-Star Team. They'd seen me get hit at the game. The coach presented me with a baseball autographed by the entire team, wishing me well (I still have it in my bookcase).

Coach Maietta invited me to City Hall the next day to be a special guest for a large city-wide celebration honoring the team for their World Series victory. He invited me to stand with the whole team as they were honored. I got to know many of the players on that team, and we remained friends for many years. It was a wonderful gesture by Coach Maietta and the team, and I appreciated the experience more than he or anyone would ever imagine. Having Steve, the All-Star team, and Coach Maietta come to my house, was a different form of encouragement, but definitely one that had an impact on me.

In a newspaper article written by Al DeSantis the next day describing the celebration, three Billy's were mentioned—Billy Connors and Billy Masucci, both starting pitchers for the Schenectady team, and me, Billy Schultz, recognized as their honorary batboy. It was quite a thrill.

During this experience, my mom got to know a lot of moms from the Schenectady team. They told her what a great mom she was for me, which was an encouraging compliment.

****

Note: This experience inspired me to later coach Little League for fourteen years. It started when my son, Brian, played. It was very special to coach my own son and many other kids—particularly boys who had no father around and simply needed encouragement.

One coaching experience reminded me of my own tryout experience. One 13-year-old boy on my team named Mike loved to play baseball. He reminded me so much of me, just loving baseball and wanting to play, yet facing similar challenges. His father and I talked about it.

One day at a practice Mike came to me and said, "I want to try being the catcher." I was very hesitant about it at first, because I didn't know how his instincts and reflexes would respond, and I was concerned he'd get hurt. But then I thought about how I'd felt when I tried out—how my parents had let me try, and then the day the coach told me I couldn't play.

The response from his parents supported his desire to try, just as my parents' response did for me. I surprised him one day and said, "Mike, you'll catch in the next game." I could hardly keep him on the ground, he was so excited. In the game, I told our pitcher to only throw fast balls, no curve balls.

For two innings, Mike caught many pitches, made no errors, and felt like a million bucks afterward. Our entire team and his parents watched, inspired, and urged him on. To this day, when I see him he often thanks me for letting him catch that day. Mike realized after catching for two innings it probably was enough, but he just felt so good that he tried and succeeded.

Being on a baseball field, hitting ground balls to the players, talking strategy with the kids, getting them to encourage one another, and helping them realize their importance as team members was a real blessing for me. It was an opportunity for me to "give back" and to help the players understand the important lessons I'd learned as a member of a team, myself.

LOVE AFFAIR WITH GOLF

It all started with a plastic golf club and an oversized ball. When I was a young kid, I'd spend hours out on the front lawn, swinging away at this big ball with a small stick. I had no idea what the game of golf was until much later. I just enjoyed swinging and hitting a ball—swatting and hitting it anywhere. It was the beginning of my love for this game I've played my entire life.

Dad also loved to play golf, and usually played with friends on Saturday mornings. He let me play with one of his golf clubs in the yard but, of course, they were way too long and heavy for me. As I got taller, I began to swing at plastic golf balls just trying to make contact. I'd play a game of hitting the ball around the outside of the house until I made a complete circle.

Aunt Mickey and Uncle Teen also loved the game, and they played it well. They belonged to a country club in Rome, New York. During one trip to visit them when I was 10, Aunt Mickey asked me to walk along with her on one of her rounds of golf. The course was a mass of green—very beautiful—and we were among the few people out that day.

As she walked toward the tee of a hole to hit her drive, she pulled out a golf ball, gave me a club, and said, "It's time for you to learn how to play golf." I was so excited, but I wasn't exactly sure what to do or how to stand. Aunt Mickey gave me a quick lesson on a proper stance and where I should position the ball in relation to my body.

Because my small left hand had only three little fingers and my arm was abnormally short, I couldn't grip the club with a standard golf grip. Instead, Aunt Mickey showed me how to hold the club with a type of baseball grip—with hands separated—so I could get a good grip on it. I remember her saying to me, "Just swing at it like you'd swing at a baseball, and hit it."

She let me use a tee on every shot, which made it easier for me to hit the ball. It was very difficult at first, trying to figure out how to grip the club with my left hand and keep the hand on the club on my follow-through. I'd swing through and my left hand would let go because that arm was much shorter. It took me a few holes, but little by little I was able to keep both hands on the club and make contact with the golf ball. She was very patient with me, always encouraging, and continually saying, "Keep your eye on the ball." As I became more successful at making contact with the golf ball, I was more excited about playing. At the time, I didn't care where or how far the ball went. I just cared about hitting it.

I was now smitten with the game. At home, I used one of dad's irons. I choked up on the club so it was the right length for me, and hit plastic balls for many hours. I kept trying to figure out a grip that would work better for the left hand, and a swing that would allow my left arm to consistently stay connected with the club on follow-through. Like every golfer, but with unique physiological challenges, I was the one who had to adapt and find a way to make it work.

On the next visit to Aunt Mickey's house, I couldn't wait to play golf, and she was very willing to take me out. Getting set to hit a shot on a fairway, I pulled out a golf tee and began to place the ball. Aunt Mickey came over, took the tee out of the ground, and proclaimed, "I think you're ready to hit the ball without a tee." I was not happy, but what she was now teaching me was how to take the same swing and the same fundamentals, and hit the ball off the ground.

After a few difficult shots and many misses, I became discouraged. But Aunt Mickey made me keep at it, cheering me on the entire time. I soon learned I could hit the ball off the ground just as well as off a tee. She was such a great encourager and coach. To this day, I think of her often whenever I play a round of golf. She knew I could do it, and she wanted me to believe it, as well. She was determined to teach me—to promote an attitude of trying, failing, trying, and eventually succeeding. I learned not to give up—to keep working at a challenge— which builds self-confidence.

Until the summer of 1958, as I approached the age of 13, the only golf I'd played was at my aunt's course. Dad played in a weekly phone company league and occasionally at a municipal course. Many of my parents' friends, including the Emery's, also played golf and were members at a local country club, The Edison Club. It was established by General Electric (GE) in 1903 for use by employees of the local plant. The golf course was well-maintained and included 27 holes, many of which were tree-lined. It was a beautiful layout.

In the early '50s, membership opened up to non-GE families. In 1957, after witnessing my new and growing interest in golf, my parents decided to apply for membership. It wasn't exactly within their budget. I don't think they would have joined if it weren't for my interest. My dad, however, was very excited to be able to play more often! A selling point for Mom was the new swimming pool right next to the golf course. She and I both loved to swim and that was another great physical activity for me.

We were put on a waiting list because only a certain percentage of members could be non-GE members. In the spring of 1958, when our family was accepted, I didn't get excited at first…until I learned that my best friend, Jimmy, had taken lessons and enjoyed playing golf. I was very excited when I found out my dad had bought a new set of clubs and I would inherit his old ones. I now had my own clubs, and I had grown tall enough to use them.

The club offered a junior membership for children under age 18 or in college. Junior golfers could play on weekdays until late afternoon, unaccompanied by an adult, and on weekend afternoons with one adult. My mom and Jimmy's mom bought junior memberships for us and put everything together to enable us to play. They took turns driving us to the club early in the morning, and picking us up late in the afternoon. Our parents loved it, because they knew where we were, enjoying our summer days. It provided them free time for themselves, as well.

For all of my teenage years, until I went off to college, every summer day was filled with golf or swimming. Jimmy and I would play either nine or 18 holes in the morning, grab lunch on the clubhouse patio, go up to the pool to swim for a while, and sometimes play nine more holes afterward. If we were too tired to play another nine, we'd go out to the practice putting green for putting contests. Soon, we met another boy in our neighborhood, Corky Kallas, who enjoyed golf, and we became a steady threesome. Other junior golfers, many of whom were schoolmates, also played with us.

Because of my arm and leg and unconventional grip, I had to work continuously on hand-eye coordination and weight transfer—creating a swing where I could maintain my balance, while turning my shoulders and hitting the ball with some power. Eventually, power was the most difficult thing to improve. The guys I played with were always outdriving me, but they'd also be in the rough, in the sand traps, or facing difficult shots. If I could keep it in the fairway, I had a chance to score as well as they could. I really had to depend on accuracy.

My key advantage was my putting and chipping, and I spent extra time on the practice green. I knew I had to be better than anyone else in those areas to be competitive. I also spent time hitting golf ball after golf ball, improving my swing, and learning how to change the swing to be more accurate and to hit the ball well. I practiced in the backyard (with plastic balls), at the corner lot up the street from our house, at the high school, and at the country club.

One day, the club pro, Bob Haggerty, was watching me swing. He took some interest in me. At first, he tried to convince me to play left-handed. Hitting right-handed, a golfer's power comes from the left arm, the lead arm of your swing. In my case, my power had to come from my right arm. He felt that, if I hit left-handed, my strong right arm, now the lead arm, would produce more power. Swinging left-handed, however, required me to release my left hand from the club on my follow-through, because that arm couldn't extend that far. I tried, but it didn't feel right.

Bob then gave me the best advice: "Bill, you have to adapt to the way that's most comfortable for you." That's the same advice my aunt had given me when I first started playing. What Bob did teach me was the rhythm of the swing, the importance of concentration, and how temperament affects your game.

Golf was very important to me because I loved to play and I also loved being with my friends. One summer day, my hip lock broke and we had to leave the leg at Mr. Dickinson's shop for a few days. I was disappointed, because I could see myself sitting home while my buddies were at the course.

I came up with an idea that my mom thought was crazy. I knew I could balance myself on one leg for many minutes if I had to. My idea was to rent a golf cart and drive up to where I would hit the ball. I'd address the ball standing on one leg and hit it. I'd use my crutches when I putted on the green. I showed my mom in the backyard how it would work, and convinced her to let me try at the golf course. The next few days, I was out again playing with my friends. My idea was a success. No one could believe it, but I played reasonably well. That just shows how much I wanted to play.

Playing as much golf as we did, my friends and I were bound to get better. Competition among the group happened constantly. But we also helped each other by always trying to play our best. All of us got to the place where we could shoot in the mid-80s for 18 holes. Some of us, including myself, had the opportunity to play on the club's junior team and play matches against other clubs.

Another key thing we had to learn was golf etiquette and proper behavior on the course. The club had a starter named Andy, a retired GE employee, who made sure players teed off on time and kept pace with groups in front of them. He took a real liking to kids and had the patience to go with it. He instructed us on how to act, when to be silent, and other important tips on behavior. Sometimes, we goofed off or acted improperly, and he'd take us aside and explain the privilege we had to play each day. He told us not to abuse it, and pointed out how our actions were affecting other people. He taught us to respect club rules and to be courteous to others. I learned from him that golf is truly a "gentlemen's game."

I had a terrific temper at times growing up, especially if I lost at something. With golf, you're really competing against the course with the challenge of maintaining a positive mindset. At times when I got very upset over a misplayed shot or a bad bounce, I'd slam my club to the ground and promptly hit another poor shot.

One day, while playing with my parents, I started hitting some errant shots. I slammed my club to the ground. Dad first encouraged me to keep trying, but then he got upset over my tantrums. "One more outburst, and I'm taking your clubs away", he said. Predictably, I hit a poor shot on the next hole and I slammed my club into my bag. Dad said nothing until we got to the car.

The next morning, my clubs were out of sight. I was very angry, but I began to realize anger didn't help and that I wasn't much fun to be around when I threw tantrums. I didn't get the clubs back for a couple of days, which really hurt. Dad reminded me, as he had several times before: "The angrier you get, the higher your score." It was a tough lesson to learn, and one I remind myself to this day when I'm on the course.

Another gratifying aspect of all this was Mom's newfound appreciation of golf at the age of 50. She realized if she didn't join in she'd become a "golf widow," with dad and me out at the course. Mom learned how to play and ended up enjoying it. Every Sunday afternoon, the three of us had a standing date to play nine holes.

Mom also met many women with whom she regularly played golf during the week, and they became good friends. It was common to see her on the clubhouse porch, after a round of golf, enjoying lunch with her friends and having a glass of sherry. Whenever the group saw me, they made me come over to chat. Mom always beamed a big smile.

Golf, and my ability to do it well, opened up many great experiences for me throughout my life. After graduating from college, I decided one year to play in the National Amputee Golf Tournament in New Jersey. I thought I was a very good golfer, given my circumstances, and thought I'd do well. I was one of the youngest participants. During a practice round leading up to the tournament, I played in a foursome: two veterans who'd each lost a limb, a man with two artificial arms, and me. In front of us was a foursome that included a young man with two short arms that stopped just below the elbows.

My first impression with these golfers was their passion toward the game. They took it very seriously, yet they enjoyed themselves. We all had to adapt in different ways in order to hit the ball. My next impression was how well they played. The man with the two artificial arms won the double amputee division of the tournament, while the young man with the two short arms shot a 78 in one round.

Needless to stay, I was humbled and inspired by these men. I averaged a score of 88 for my four 18-hole rounds—a score I was happy with, yet it only placed me in the middle of the pack. It was a great experience for me—reinforcing how the human spirit can help you achieve goals that seem beyond your reach.

Later, I had the opportunity to attend business meetings while working for GE that included playing beautiful golf courses with customers. The venues in Puerto Rico, Florida, Georgia, and California were challenging, and the scenery was breathtaking. I met and got to know many wonderful people in my business career while playing golf. And I even had a job interview playing a round of golf. (I got the job.)

Friendships formed and solidified while playing golf—starting with my days at The Edison Club as a young boy, playing with Jimmy and Corky; and later, as an adult after becoming a club member on my own. In recent years—more than 30 years since we worked together—a group of GE friends have regularly invited me to their annual golf outing in Myrtle Beach, South Carolina. From the moment I arrived the first time, it felt like we hadn't skipped a beat—enjoying each other's company and trading barbs and old stories.

During the past 20 years, I've been in a golf league with men from my church. Golf brought us together, and helped us build lifelong friendships.

As a father, I wanted to teach my young son, Brian, the things I'd enjoyed. When he was very young, we gave him a plastic golf club and ball, just like my parents had for me. I watched Brian swat at the ball, miss it, swat at it again, and then begin to hit it regularly. As I watched, I reflected back on the days when I had hit the plastic ball, over and over, around our house.

As Brian grew up, he took a few lessons and off he went, becoming an excellent golfer. It's still a joy to play with him, even though he beats me (in spite of his inability to hit fairways). Just playing golf with my son makes me feel like a winner. I was able to pass on my enthusiasm for a great game that has had a profound impact on my life.

A PART OF THE TEAM

When I started playing all those backyard games as a small child, my vision was that I would be able to play the games for the rest of my life. At one point, I actually was one of the better baseball players in the entire neighborhood, and I also played very competitively in basketball and football. In spite of people telling me I wouldn't be able to do this or that when I got older, I just didn't believe it. I was as good as anybody else and I enjoyed it, so why not?

In a way, it was fortunate that my parents let me learn on my own that there might come a time when I couldn't play some sports any longer. But I resisted thinking along those lines. I'd seen how sports helped me enjoy life. Athletics gave me a very healthy level of self-esteem and self-confidence, based on success fueled by a competitive spirit. These have helped me overcome many things—especially when life events became very difficult or when I needed to convince someone I could, indeed, do the job.

As I entered Van Antwerp Junior High for seventh grade, I began to realize I really couldn't run as fast as my friends anymore. As hard as I tried, it was becoming apparent that the gap between their speed and mine was getting wider. It made me sad to realize the backyard games would never be the same. The friendships that grew out of those games over those years were great gifts. Realizing I could no longer play baseball with any of my friends was hard to accept.

I still felt I was as good as my friends when it came to skills (for example, batting, throwing, and catching), but the running part became the issue. Running with one good leg and a full prosthesis on the other began to limit me when it came to increasing my speed. Keeping up with other boys simply wasn't going to happen anymore.

Jimmy and the other guys who were good athletes turned their attention to tryouts for the junior high basketball and baseball teams. Mom and Dad tried to console me as this realization became apparent to me. But for a long time, my sadness prevailed. Playing sports had made me the confident kid I was, and now some of the more popular sports I loved to play—baseball, basketball, and football—were games I could no longer play with my friends. I'd excelled at most sports and my friends respected me for my skills as much as my will to play. What would they think now? Would we still get together and play games? Would we still remain good friends? I didn't cry on the outside but it was tearing me up inside.

I wasn't finished trying, though. My school had two major varsity sports: basketball and baseball. It was one of three major junior high schools in the city, and had a strong tradition of winning teams. Though I realized I was having more trouble keeping up with other guys, my heart led me to try out for the basketball team. Mom and Dad tried to convince me it might not be a good idea but I had to try. I needed to find out for myself. I could shoot better than most of my friends, I was a great passer, and I thought I could keep up if I worked harder.

On the first day of tryouts, my outside shooting went very well. I made a very high percentage of my outside shots and foul shots. I played pretty good defense. But running a full court, instead of playing in someone's driveway, was quite different and really hard for me. I was tired when I got home. My parents were a little surprised that I'd gone through with it. I felt good about myself, and about my effort.

The next day, before tryouts started, the head coach, Mr. Ciabotti, asked to speak with me. He told me how impressed he was in my trying out—the effort I was putting into it, and how inspiring it was to watch me. He looked me in the eye and said, "I want you to be a part of the team, but as the student manager. We need you on this team." He explained the reason—the same one I'd heard during Little League tryouts: "You might get hurt or you might hurt someone."

I was very disappointed. I told him I'd think about it. The reality of it all began to hit me hard. I went from feeling angry to being sad, and back to being angry again. My competitive drive said, "Don't give up, you can do it. You are as good a player as anyone else trying out."

But I knew deep down I wouldn't be able to keep up. I just didn't want to accept it.

The fact that he wanted me on the team, though, was great to hear. Being on a team with my friends was important to me. I didn't want to be sitting up in the bleachers watching. I wanted to be with my friends on the team! I could tell my friends on the team were happy when I told the coach I wanted to do it. And my parents weren't just happy, they were relieved. Coming to that conclusion myself, rather than just accepting someone else's opinion, made it easier for me. Yes, I felt some sadness, but I felt better about myself for trying. As Aunt Mickey told me, "You succeeded by trying."

That spring, when baseball tryouts started, I was tempted to try out again. I dreamed of playing centerfield on the team—just like my dream of playing for the Yankees in Yankee Stadium. I loved playing baseball: the hitting, fielding, throwing, running—every aspect of it. But, instead, I made the difficult decision to ask the coach about being the student manager. He was thrilled and supportive. He even let me field ground balls or catch fly balls during practice.

As a student manager, I had many responsibilities—most of them thankless, dirty jobs like picking up dirty uniforms and towels, retrieving balls, unpacking and packing equipment, keeping statistics for the coach, and keeping score at games. During practices, I watched and listened to the coach when he talked to the players, and I joined in when he shouted encouragement to them. I felt like I was an important part of the team and helping them succeed. I had found my niche. I could be part of the team and contribute in a different way.

In the fall of 1959, I entered ninth grade at Niskayuna High School—one of several new high schools built in the mid-1950s to meet the area's increasing population. Niskayuna High School was located adjacent to my neighborhood, which made it convenient. I walked up my street, through a path in a wooded area, past the football field, and into the building.

The previous spring, the high school had had an orientation day for the incoming freshmen class. We got a tour of the entire building, which was on one level with long, sprawling hallways. We also got to meet many of the teachers we'd have during the next four years. That day, during lunch, a man approached our table and sat down next to me. He introduced himself as Coach Don Boothe—the head football coach. He said he'd heard about me and my love for sports from the junior high coaches. He went on to talk about the high school's football team, and his desire to have students on the team who not only showed ability but also character. He then surprised me by saying, "You're the type of young man I want on my team. You inspire your teammates. I want you to be the student manager, if you're interested."

I was shocked beyond belief. I immediately said, "Yes." What a great feeling it was to be not only accepted and included on the football team—but even sought out! I couldn't wait to tell my friends and my parents. During my four years on the team, Coach Boothe became a mentor: He inspired me and taught me many life principles. I always looked up to him. In addition to being a great person, Coach Boothe was a great coach—guiding the team to the league title four years in a row.

The other assistant coaches, many of whom were also my teachers, also inspired me to be the best student manager I could be and to contribute to the team as much as possible. They'd heard about my interest in statistics and had me take stats during each game, including listing each play and the results from the play. I learned the entire playbook and started anticipating the play calls coach would make. Coach Boothe and his staff used the play history and stats I accumulated to set the game plan for an upcoming game. I felt like I was a coach!

Soon after I started ninth grade, I was introduced to Coach Tom Howley, the basketball coach, and Coach Jim Shea, the baseball coach. They also asked me if I'd be interested in being student manager for those teams—starting with the freshmen teams and moving to junior varsity and varsity teams as I progressed. I was so excited about being a member of these teams—being with my friends, experiencing the camaraderie, and continuing throughout my high-school years. We had great teams in those sports, too—winning multiple league titles in both basketball and baseball.

I learned so much from these coaches and teams that has carried over into my life. The coaches expected me, as student manager, to take on important responsibilities that would contribute to the team's success. I wasn't brought on simply as a nice gesture. The type and breadth of dirty, behind-the-scenes work I did on the junior high teams was greatly expanded in high school. I learned I was counted on to do what was asked, just like the players. At one away football game, I forgot to pack some important equipment. When he found out, Coach Boothe chewed me out in front of the entire football team. It taught me a couple of things: First, I had to take my responsibilities seriously and do them well, and second, I was an important member of the team. I wasn't only along for the ride and the experience; I was there to do a job. In a weird kind of way, his reprimand gave me a feeling of inclusion and importance.

I also learned the importance of hard work and the power of teamwork. Sitting through all the practices for all three sports, listening to the coaches, seeing the teams repeat drills day after day, working with team members as a unit, and preparing for each game made me realize how hard teams and individuals had to work to succeed. We didn't just win on skill alone. The success of our high-school teams was a result of a "team" attitude, created and fortified by the coaches.

Those four years of high school were some of the happiest years of my life. To be a part of this positive experience with some of my best friends, and with great mentorship from coaches, was beneficial beyond measure.

At the end of each school year, the high school held an all-sports banquet to recognize all the students who'd participated in team sports that year. Coaches, students, and their parents attended the banquets. Players who'd earned letters for each sport were recognized, along with those who'd displayed outstanding performance.

At my final high-school banquet my senior year, after they'd named letter winners for each sport, it dawned on me that my name hadn't been called. Other friends sitting with me mentioned it, as well. Minutes later, Coach Boothe went to the podium. He started talking about a young man he'd met four years ago as a freshman—a young man he'd gotten to know not only as a student but also like a son. He described the young man as "an inspiration to me and to everyone."

He then announced the creation of a special award, called the Varsity Award, to be given to Bill Schultz, "for his contributions as a student manager on the football, basketball, and baseball teams."

As he said my name, I went numb.

The next thing I knew, I saw everyone standing and applauding. My parents made me stand up, and said, "You'd better go up there and get your award." As I approached Coach Boothe and made eye contact with him, I saw tears of pride in his eyes, and I got misty myself. I looked at the head table and made eye contact with the other coaches. My lips said "thank you" to them. As I returned to my seat, the applause continued, and I saw Mom and Dad beaming, and Mom crying. I hugged them both. It was a fulfilling moment for them, and I told them later that the award was as much a tribute to them as it was for me.

In 2013, while writing this book, I was able to track down Coach Boothe, retired and living in Alabama. We talked by phone and shared memories of the great football teams we'd had at Niskayuna back in the early 1960s. The main reason I called him was to thank him, again, for his part and influence in my life. I needed to tell him that again, just as I had at the banquet.

A few days after we talked, I received a letter from him, which read:

"I was always impressed with your determination and infectious enthusiasm. It was not a hard decision selecting you as my varsity football manager. I expected a lot from my managers: It was a tough job. You were a heck of a manager; you took care of our team in spite of any challenges.

You became an integral part of the team. This is very hard, for the position of manager is often focused at very different tasks than the rest of the team. But you had the charisma and leadership ability to overcome that barrier. You were always inspirational and we were much better because of that."

An "integral part of the team": That was a great comment to hear and something I have strived to be throughout my life.

MY MUSICAL JOURNEY

From the time I sat by the Victrola as a two-year-old, I've always enjoyed music—whether it's singing along with a record or in a singing group, or just listening to others perform. Mom realized quite early that I enjoyed music, and she wanted to nurture that interest. As she listened to me sing along with recordings, she realized I could carry a tune.

Mom loved music herself, so my interest brought smiles to her face. She'd played piano from a young age, and sang in school chorus groups. She saw music as an activity I'd enjoy and could handle, something I would enjoy all my life.

When I entered second grade at Craig School, Miss Naylor, the school's music teacher, organized a school chorus group and Mom made sure I was in it. I wasn't as excited about it as Mom was, but I did it because it pleased her. Throughout grade school, the boys, including me, were still sopranos. We put on two concerts a year—one at Christmas and another at the end of the year. One year, I was asked to sing a solo on a Christmas song. It was a very short solo, but I was very nervous. Mom was excited about it, so I knew I couldn't back out. She said my performance was great. Throughout my school days, I enjoyed singing in groups, but the solos weren't my thing.

Mom convinced me to join our church's children's choir. (Actually, I knew I had no choice). The music had lyrics we didn't understand, sometimes in other languages such as Latin, but the harmonies were outstanding. I didn't realize, and Mom didn't tell me, we'd have to wear choir robes during the service. Imagine my surprise when I found out the robes had very large red bows on the front. We looked like "cheerful cherubs." After any church service where we sang, the adults would tap us on the head, telling us how cute we were. That was not pleasant.

Before I was old enough to play in a band, Mom showed me the trumpet my brother had played when he was in high school. He'd practiced in the house several times a week. I was interested in it after hearing him play. I loved the sound of brass. I'd seen Louis Armstrong and other trumpeters play on television, and the sound was impressive. When Mom asked me to try it, though, we discovered a trumpet was too long for me to hold it up with my short left arm.

Mom knew about the cornet—a shorter, more compact instrument similar to a trumpet. I was able to hold it comfortably with my left hand cradled underneath. She was able to find one for sale and lined me up for lessons. (I didn't like that part— it meant I had to practice!) I started taking weekly lessons, and began practicing every day—building up my lip and learning the scales. As I got better, the drudgery of it all lessened and I began enjoying the sound of the cornet. I began to play songs off sheet music.

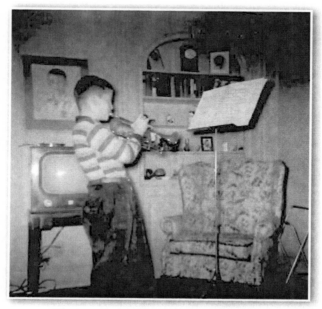

Playing the cornet at my aunt's house

In junior high, I signed up for chorus and band. Everyone who wanted to be a part of those groups could. It was a fun experience and I looked forward to doing the same thing in high school.

In high school, tryouts were required for the choir and the band because they were so popular, and many kids didn't make the cut. My years of singing, on the living room floor and in the children's choirs, gave me a lot of confidence. And all the cornet lessons and the practice I hadn't looked forward to paid off. As a result, I had successful band and choir tryouts.

The choral director's name was Miss Mooney. Kids loved her because she made choir fun, even though she "pushed" us to keep improving and to sing songs correctly. She was tough, but we all knew she cared about us. She'd get outwardly angry when we didn't take practice seriously. She demanded excellence. She'd even stop us in the middle of a song, during a concert, and make us start over. The results of her leadership and influence showed in our performances. I sang the second tenor part, which was a harmonizing part. Miss Mooney helped me develop my voice and nurtured my desire to sing the best I could. She was another encourager in my life.

In high school, we had what was called the Symphonic Band—with strings, brass, and percussion. The director, Mr. Schiff, was a very funny guy who knew how to get the best out of us. He challenged us with difficult music. He'd yell to get our attention, and then start smiling. Since I played the cornet, which gave off a mellower tone than the trumpet, I played harmony in the background. The highlight of the year was the Christmas concert, which we always ended with Leroy Anderson's rendition of "Sleigh Ride."

In high school, the students put on a talent show every year, and I was invited to join a group performing a song from the musical, "Bye Bye Birdie." I played a nerdy guy who had a solo line that brought laughter and applause.

Mom and Dad took me to New York City a couple of times to see Broadway musicals. I wasn't keen about going, but they told me that the first musical I saw, "Damn Yankees," was about the New York Yankees.

I also saw "I Do, I Do," with Gordon McRae and Carol Lawrence. Mom took me to musicals made into movies, such as "Showboat" "Carousel" and "Oklahoma."

Shortly after college, I heard about tryouts for the Schenectady Light Opera Company for the musical, "South Pacific." I earned a spot in the chorus, a group of Navy sailors. Later, I had a talking and singing part in "How to Succeed in Business Without Even Trying." The quality of the performances by this group was outstanding.

Mom was pleased that I was involved in music. It all started with the little Victrola on our living room floor, followed by the experiences and opportunities she introduced me to. I've enjoyed music all my life—whether being on the stage, in the audience, or simply listening to all types of music on the radio. She was right: Music has been an experience I've enjoyed throughout my life.

ADOLESCENCE AND GIRLS

As I grew into adolescence, the thought that I might not be accepted, included, or considered a friend crept into my mind. As I began to fall farther behind, physically and athletically, I wondered if my friends would continue to include me as I moved into my junior and senior high-school years.

It was very important for me, like any adolescent, to be accepted by peers, to be popular, and to be part of a socially acceptable group. Until adolescence, I'd never had any doubts whatsoever about being included in anything. Certainly, being part of the sports teams helped me. My friends, however, began paying more attention to the socializing part of school, and their natural attraction to girls began. I started to think there were fun things going on that I wasn't a part of any longer.

Starting in 8th grade, Saturday night school dances in the gym were the place to be, with local disc-jockeys playing records and lots of dancing going on. "Sock Hops" after basketball games were fun because you didn't need a date. I certainly wanted to be a part of the dancing scene.

A year or two before junior high, my mom signed me up for a dancing class at a local studio. About 10 girls and 10 boys my age were in the class. At the time, a few of the popular dances were "The Stroll" and "The Twist," along with slow-dancing numbers. I was a pretty good dancer, and I enjoyed it.

By high school, my biggest fear was asking a girl to dance or asking one out on a date. My confidence level wasn't the same as it was playing sports. At that age, kids were attracted to the most handsome guy or the prettiest girl. Personality, or the fact that you were a nice person, was secondary. I started to think about what I looked like physically: a guy with one leg, a short arm, and wearing glasses. I was far from the guy girls wanted to date or found attractive. Would a girl even go out with me? Would I go through school without ever having a date? I was feeling insecure about this new social aspect of life.

But those thoughts didn't hold me back from asking out the prettiest and most popular girls first. And they usually rejected me. I got a lot of "no's," although they didn't stop me from asking. One girl I'd asked out a few times said, "Bill, you need to stop asking me out because I really don't have an interest in going out with you." That was almost better to hear than, "I'd love to, but I already have a date," or "I'm not going to the dance," and then seeing the girl at the dance with another guy. That really hurt.

My mom always asked me, "Why are you asking this girl out? Why don't you ask out other nice girls?" Like other kids my age, I was guilty of looking at the outside of a person.

But I do know that whenever I had a date, we always had fun. We danced a lot—to both fast and slow songs. Maybe these girls thought of me as the kind of date they knew wouldn't go anywhere; that it was just for fun.

I did enjoy dancing, which made the social scene a little easier. Most boys at that age didn't like to fast dance, so I was busy with dance partners. Usually, the dance floor was filled with girls dancing with each other. When a slow song started playing, the boys rushed the floor with their dates.

The dates I did have were fun, including the junior and senior proms. I always had a date, but I never "went steady" or dated the same person for very long. I was like any other guy attracted to beautiful girls. But I also learned that personality was important. I began noticing girls who weren't necessarily partygoers, but who were friendly and fun to be around.

I really enjoyed being with one girl I took to a dance in eighth grade. She was the sister of one of my best friends. She hung around our Little League games, since she lived right across the street from the field. She was cute and she loved sports, especially baseball. We always had some good laughs when we were together. We talked over the phone some nights. With this girl, I started to get a sense of what a healthy relationship might be like.

Certainly, I had normal adolescent doubts. But those doubts turned out to be more of an issue to me than anyone else. I wasn't into the party scene and, at the time, I felt like I wasn't part of the "in crowd." There were moments when I felt sad that I wasn't included, but I eventually felt comfortable with the way it was.

I soon realized I didn't need to be in the "in crowd" to be liked and to feel good about myself. Team sports filled that need. I had plenty of friends and two parents at home who loved me. When I think back, I realize I was part of the group I wanted to associate with, and I suppose a lot of it had to do with simply being myself.

COLLEGE CHOICES

During Dad's senior year in high school, he received a football scholarship offer from Rutgers University in New Brunswick, New Jersey. He was an offensive lineman and captain of the high-school football team. He was also the team's field-goal kicker. In that era, the football was slightly rounder, and the kicker drop-kicked it—with the ball actually hitting the ground before the kicker kicked it. For many years, Dad held the record for the longest field goal (50 yards) in the DUSO (Dutchess/Ulster/Sullivan/Orange County) League in upstate New York.

Dad was one of the best athletes in the school. The scholarship would have paid for his entire four-year college education, and would have enabled him to be the first person in the family to graduate from college. At the time, his father, Grandpa Wally, traveled almost every day of the week working for the railroad. When his mother became an invalid and wheelchair-bound, she needed care regularly throughout the day—care that, for the most part, was her son's (my dad's) responsibility. As a result, my dad had to make one of the most difficult decisions of his life. He had to turn down the scholarship offer to stay home and care for his mom.

One of Dad's best friends at the time was a man named Willard "Bill" Sahloff. Bill was also Dad's teammate in three sports—football, basketball, and baseball. When Dad received the scholarship offer from Rutgers, Bill was also being considered for that same scholarship. Because Dad had to turn down the scholarship offer, Bill was awarded the scholarship in his place.

Bill Sahloff went on to graduate from Rutgers, and later became vice president of General Electric Company's housewares division. In that position, he conceived the electric toothbrush and the electric knife product ideas, and he built the housewares business into one of the largest and most profitable divisions within the company.

Years later, Bill Sahloff offered a special gift to my dad, and I was the recipient.

In the fall of 1961, at the start of my junior year in high school, my parents and I started getting serious about my college plans. Most of our focus was on colleges in New York State. We visited larger schools like Cornell and Syracuse, but both campuses were very hilly. And we visited smaller schools like Hamilton College and Colgate. Both of those schools had beautiful, level campuses, and weren't far from where my aunt and uncle lived. But all of these schools were very expensive and probably not affordable for my parents.

But then something happened at Colgate. Every fall, when I was growing up, Mom, Dad, and I went to a Colgate football game and tailgating party with my aunt and uncle. The adults enjoyed tailgating before the game and usually met up with other friends. Those days were typically beautiful—with the fall colors and crisp air.

On a late November day in 1961, Colgate was playing Rutgers. It was a cold, windy day with a touch of snow in the air. During the game, as we were sitting up in the stands, my mom spotted a rather large man in a red plaid coat and hat walking along in front of our section of the bleachers. She kept looking at him, thinking he looked familiar. She turned to my dad and said, "I think that man is Bill Sahloff." Bill had been an enthusiastic supporter of Rutgers athletics ever since he'd graduated, and he rarely missed a football game. My mom encouraged my dad to walk down the bleachers and see if it was Bill. He hadn't seen his friend for more than 30 years.

Dad rather reluctantly strode down the bleacher steps and caught up with him. As soon as they looked at each other—sure enough, it was Bill Sahloff. They shook hands, patted each other on the shoulder, and then started talking. Mom and I just watched, and noticed Bill eventually was doing all the talking and Dad was simply nodding. Dad eventually returned to his seat, and both of us saw in his face that whatever Bill said had really touched him.

As they were talking, Dad had pointed us out to Bill and we waved back. When Dad got back to us, he explained that Bill had asked Dad about me, and Dad told him my story in brief. Bill then started to talk to Dad at length. What he said was, "Schultzie, I still appreciate what you did for your mom, which gave me the opportunity to go to Rutgers. I want to do something for you and your son, Billy. I want him to consider Rutgers for college. I'm on the Board of Trustees there and I'll write a letter of recommendation on his behalf. Would you please ask him to consider the school?"

Rutgers previously hadn't been on our minds as a potential college for me, but now it was. Bill Sahloff recommended we visit the campus and talk to the people in admissions. Since Rutgers was the state school of New Jersey, only a small percentage of out-of-state applicants were accepted. My high-school grades were OK—about a B average—so acceptance wasn't automatic, by any means.

But we decided to visit, if only to check it out. Mom and I really liked the campus. Established in 1766, the school had many beautiful, older buildings with a beautiful, grassy quad and tree-lined walkways. And another plus—while it was large, it was relatively flat, which would make it easier for walking.

Since we liked the school and the campus, I completed my application and Bill Sahloff sent in his recommendation letter. He sent us a copy, which Mom and Dad found heart-warming.

We didn't hear back for a couple of months.

I began to have my heart set on Rutgers, but my parents, in the meantime, had linked up with the New York State Division of Vocational Rehabilitation (DVR) to determine if there was any financial support available for them to help pay for my college expenses. Because of my disability, I was eligible for assistance from the state if it was determined that I met certain criteria.

We visited the state DVR offices and met with Don Morelli, one of the counselors. Don was a pleasant man in his mid-30s. He had a genuine desire to help us, and took me through all the necessary steps to determine any eligibility for financial aid. As it was a state agency, its typical financial aid award would be for attending a New York state college. Don was aware of my desire to go to Rutgers, but tried to convince me that the state colleges might be an alternative if financial aid was available.

I sensed that the financial load for my parents was going to be rather significant, and I was aware they were concerned about their ability to pay for my schooling. One other possibility in addition to a state college was the University of Illinois, which had a special program for people with physical disabilities. New York State and the State of Illinois had some kind of reciprocal agreement through which I could attend Illinois as an out-of-state student and get a full scholarship from New York State.

But when my mom heard that the program segregated handicapped students from the rest of the student body, she immediately reacted by saying, "That wouldn't be the best thing for Bill. He needs to be with the rest of the student body, regardless of his situation." I was so happy and relieved when she said that. Don, hearing her concerns, and knowing me, totally agreed. Yet it would have taken a huge financial burden off my parents' shoulders if I'd gone to Illinois. Instead, they looked out for my best interests and sacrificed financially.

Mom learned that Don was an avid golfer, and they talked about my golfing interest and ability. Don was very interested in playing a round of golf with me.

I remember the day we first played golf together at the Edison Club. Don was tall—6'4" and 250 pounds—and could hit the ball a mile. But after 18 holes and adding up the score, I had beaten him by several strokes. We sat on the country club porch for a burger afterward, and he just looked at me and said, "Bill, I can't believe how well you play the game of golf." I think that really helped him understand that Illinois—with its policy of segregating those with disabilities from the main student body—wasn't the right fit for me.

What he did next was extraordinary.

He realized that Rutgers was my first choice (if I was accepted), and he petitioned the DVR to make a formal exception in my case to grant financial aid for me to go to an out-of-state school like Rutgers. I know Don met a lot of resistance in doing it, but he felt strongly enough to persist, and he eventually got the approval for us. The compromise was that we didn't get all the financial aid we normally would have received, but a good portion of my tuition would be paid for under the DVR program.

About a year later, Don and his wife decided to join the Edison Club, and we soon became occasional golf buddies and good friends. We kept in touch throughout my college years, and a few years thereafter, and I think Don was as proud of my accomplishments as my parents were.

Don was another person in a line of many who came along and helped in an extraordinary way.

The long-anticipated news came in the mail in March of my senior year of high school. An envelope with the return address "Rutgers College, Office of Admissions" arrived. Since we hadn't heard anything for nearly three months, we'd begun to think I wouldn't be accepted. In fact, we were considering other schools as possibilities.

The envelope was a little thicker than normal. Mom wanted me to open it. As I opened it and unfolded the letter, I thought about the first sentence of the letter. Would it start with, "We are sorry to inform you..." or "We are happy to inform you..."?

As I read that first sentence, I couldn't help but smile and Mom immediately knew. "I'm accepted," I yelled. Mom and I had such a long embrace. She was so happy and the tears in her eyes were happy ones. It was great to see her so pleased. The years and hours of sacrifices she and Dad had made for me were being rewarded.

When Dad got home, I showed him the acceptance letter. The expression on his face was pure satisfaction and joy: I would be able to do what he was unable to, thanks to a bond with an old friend.

That night, Mom and Dad called Bill Sahloff to thank him. He already knew I was accepted, and he was as happy as my folks. In his mind, he'd returned a favor that had changed the course of his own life.

LEAVING HOME

Before I knew it, it was time to start packing and preparing for college. Rutgers, located in northern New Jersey, was about four hours by bus from home. I realized now that I'd be on my own.

Throughout my entire life until this point, Mom had always taken care of the many details of my life—like cleaning my clothes, making my bed, making arrangements for transportation, getting me to and from places, pushing me to get my homework done, and essentially guiding me and telling me what I needed to do. I was pretty spoiled.

Realizing it was now time for me to learn how to do many of these things on my own, she put me through "summer training." She showed me how to do my laundry, fold sheets, and organize my clothes among other important details. She wanted me to learn how to live independently.

Mom always thought ahead and was very practical regarding my care—she made sure I was signed up for a dorm room, bed linens, and meal plans. She even tried to show me how to make a tie knot, for occasions when I might have to dress up. That experiment failed but, fortunately, "clip-on" ties came into vogue at that point.

Mom even made sure there was a prosthetics lab nearby. Fortunately, there was one right in town, within walking distance of campus.

I suppose all this preparation kept her mind off the fact that very soon I wouldn't be living at home. In late August 1963, my parents drove me to school. When we got there, we unpacked and moved my belongings into my dorm room, which I shared with Ken Heffner, another freshman, who turned out to be a great roommate.

One of my life's most difficult moments came next.

As we headed back to the car, I realized I'd be on my own, in a new setting, a distance from home and my parents. My dad wished me the best, and got in the car—not showing the emotions and the sense of pride he was feeling. But Mom teared up and I did the same.

Mom's tears were ones of both happiness and sadness:

- Happiness, because of what I had become, because I was starting college, and because I was able to live and function on my own due to the sacrifices my parents had made, the trials they'd gone through, and the love and encouragement they'd given me.
- Sadness, because I was leaving home, and would be too far away to visit very often. Perhaps it brought back memories of leaving me off at the hospital as a child.

As the car drove off and turned the corner, Mom and I caught each other's eyes and waved. I couldn't hold back the tears. As I walked back to my dorm, memories rushed through my mind—all the things my parents had done to get me to this point. And interests and experiences my parents had exposed me to, which would spur me on to pursue them. My tears turned to smiles: I was on my own, starting a new chapter in my life. But my parents were always in my thoughts.

I got busy right away. I wanted to be a student manager in the football program at Rutgers because of the positive experience I'd had in high school, and because it would allow me to continue involvement on a team. Coach Boothe, my high school coach, wrote a glowing recommendation to John Bateman, Rutgers' head football coach who, in turn, wrote me a letter inviting me to freshman football practice. Coach Bateman liked my attitude and, after I was part of the freshman team my first year, he encouraged me to serve for three years as the student manager on the varsity football team.

This activity brought many benefits—including building friendships with great guys who loved sports and were experiencing the same feelings and challenges I was—away from home and taking on responsibility with our studies. These new friendships also led me to join Phi Gamma Delta fraternity, which at Rutgers included mostly football players and other athletes. I also became a student manager of the varsity lacrosse team in the spring.

During my years as student manager of the football team, Mom and Dad made the trip to Rutgers for many home football games. In addition to visiting me, they also joined in on Bill Sahloff's tailgating parties before and after the game. Bill and Dad had a lot of catching up to do. I always made it a point to go over and say hello to Bill and his wife, Margaret, after the game. They took a genuine interest in me throughout my college years. They had no children of their own, and funded several athletic scholarships for many years. They called the student/athletes who received the funding "their boys," and they included me in that category. Every year, Bill took all of us (by limousine) to New York City to attend the annual College Football Hall of Fame Dinner at the Waldorf Astoria. That was a thrill! It was great to know the Sahloffs, and gratifying to see Dad hooking up with his old high-school friend.

One memory on the football team stands out, because of an experience earlier in my childhood. In 1957, when I was 12, Dad took me to see Army play The University of Utah at West Point. The pageantry and the parades were wonderful and very patriotic. I told Dad at the time I wanted to go to college there. I remember sitting in the stadium as the teams ran on the field, and then as the West Point cadets began singing their fight song, "On, Brave Old Army Team." It gave me goosebumps. Army won a thrilling game, with a final score of 39-33.

Fast forward to 1963, my freshman year at Rutgers: As I scanned the future football schedules, I noticed Rutgers would play Army at West Point in the fall of '65, my junior year. I couldn't wait for that day.

I got my parents tickets to the game. I was so excited—looking forward to running on the field with the team. Usually, I stayed near the back when the team took to the field. But on that day, I was near the front. I don't think I'd run that fast since childhood baseball games in my backyard. What an exciting experience!

We put up a valiant effort against a stronger Army team and lost that day, 23-6, but the memory will always be with me.

Another thing that kept me busy right from the start was the Rutgers Glee Club. When I'd read Rutgers' admissions brochure, an article about the Glee Club described how the group had just returned from a tour of Europe. It showed photos of the students dressed in formal tails and blazers. The article piqued my interest, and I found out students had to audition at the start of freshman year, with only a select few chosen to join.

The Glee Club's long-time music director was "Soup" Walter, whom I remember fondly. He ran the auditions. I remember him giving me sheet music for three different songs, and asking me to sing the tenor part while he played the piano.

Talk about being nervous—I was shaking inside. Fortunately, I could read music, and the vocal training I'd learned from my childhood music teacher, Miss Mooney, helped me to sing confidently and on tune. We had to wait a few days to find out if we were chosen. When I saw the posted list of new members with my name on it, I immediately called Mom. She was thrilled. Actually, I was happier for her than for myself. The first call she made was to Miss Mooney to tell her the news.

Being selected meant I needed Mom's sewing help right away. For our concerts, we wore formal tails during the first half, and gray blazers during the second half. The club sold us the tails and blazers, so I purchased mine along with everyone else. But the left arm had to be shortened on both, and the pants had to be altered. I took the bus home one weekend, and she made all the alterations in about a day. What would I do without her?!

I was in the Glee Club all four years of college, singing as a second tenor. The group included guys with many backgrounds and interests. It was good for me to move beyond friendships only with athletes, and to talk about topics other than sports. Our common interest was singing.

We were all there to sing our best. I was impressed by the sound of the group even during our first practice together. The harmony and tone were incredible, and I had that same feeling during concerts. "Soup" was demanding, just like Miss Mooney, and challenged us with difficult music—from classical to modern. He was funny, down-to-earth, and a father figure for all of us. We performed at concerts at least twice a month in the tri-state area and on campus. We also toured Europe the summer before my senior year, which was a wonderful experience and opportunity.

I'll never forget one particular heartwarming experience. One fall evening, the Glee Club members joined up with the Rutgers University Choir—which was much larger and included women from Douglass College—for a concert with the New York Symphony Orchestra at Carnegie Hall in New York City. Leopold Stokowski, a leading conductor of the 20th century, conducted the orchestra. What an honor and thrill to sing in that historic hall, and under a renowned conductor. Carnegie Hall was filled that night, and it was a marvelous experience—ending with a standing ovation.

As we left stage and entered our dressing room, two women stood off to the side. I ignored them at first, but then I looked back and saw that one of them was my mom.

I couldn't believe it! She had taken the train down from Schenectady to attend the concert and stayed with an old high-school friend who lived in the city. The joy on Mom's face was overwhelming. We both began to tear up and we embraced. Mom told me how proud she was. I looked her in the eye and said, "This happened because of your encouragement, and your desire for me to live life like anyone else." It was a defining moment for both of us.

Another great gift my parents gave me was financial support, so I didn't have to work during college. Not only was I able to concentrate on my studies, but I also was able to be active in groups like varsity football, lacrosse, Glee Club, and the Phi Gamma Delta fraternity. I was fortunate to have parents who saved and sacrificed so I could go to school without that financial burden. I know Mom and Dad couldn't really afford to pay for my Rutgers education on their own. My tuition was significantly higher as an out-of-state student. It would have been much less of a burden if I'd attended a college in New York State, but they were intent on me attending Rutgers.

REALITY STRIKES

In the fall of 1966, at the end of the football season, as I left the stadium for the last time as the team's student manager, one of my teammates said, "I guess it's time for us to start thinking about interviewing for jobs in the real world."

As we rode the bus back to the main campus, I began thinking about what he'd said and realized I needed to start thinking about my career. We'd received several notices from the career center that many companies were scheduling on-campus interviews, which were filling up fast. The following Monday, I walked down to the career center to begin researching companies to consider. Most on-campus interviews were with large, nationally known corporations.

I signed up to interview with three companies for entry-level marketing or financial positions. One company I didn't sign up for was General Electric because, quite frankly, I was fearful of having to work back in my hometown of Schenectady. It was a large GE town, and I wanted to begin my career somewhere else. I also wanted to stay away from a job at New York Telephone, where Dad and Dick worked. I had the typical attitude of wanting to prove myself on my own.

My first interview was with a large manufacturing company. I prepared for the interview by going to the library and learning more about the company. I was attracted to it because of its market leadership and size—thinking there were many career opportunities and good jobs available at the company. I walked into the interview room and met the college recruiter, a man in his 50s, who worked out of the corporate office. He greeted me with a handshake and a look I won't forget.

Before I sat down, he looked at my left hand and said, "What's wrong with your hand?" I responded, "There's really nothing wrong with my hand other than the fact that I was just born this way." He then asked me some very polite questions, but I knew right away it wasn't going to go very far. He described his company as one that required a lot of physical dexterity and ability to work in the plant. I'd thought the interview would be for marketing positions, which is how it was advertised at the career center.

Even though I emphasized my coursework in marketing and finance, it was quite apparent the recruiter had already ruled me out. He asked me a couple of times about my disabilities, and it became apparent that not only was it a company that didn't want me, but I didn't want to work for the company or the people who ran it.

That was when the reality hit that I'd face concerns and obstacles in finding and starting my career. It was the first time I can recall that my disability was the focus and my ability was questioned. The recruiter thanked me for interviewing, but made no comment about what would happen next. It was clear my disability was the reason for the lack of interest…he made that quite apparent.

As I walked back to the fraternity house, I felt dejected—not because it was a well-known company I'd wanted to work for, but because I'd been rejected and hadn't felt that way before. I was angered by his questions about my disability. I said to myself, "He judged me before he knew anything about me. I'd love to show him how physical I can be." I was steamed.

Fortunately, I had a pretty healthy level of self-esteem, so challenges in the past hadn't affected me much. This was different, though, because without knowing me as a person or my skill sets, he'd rejected me outright—simply through the questions he asked and how he asked them. His total approach to the interview was galling. Since this was my first interview, I thought, "Is this how they'll all go?"

By the time I got back to the fraternity house I was still mad and said some naughty words, but I was still determined. I prepared for my next interviews with the other companies. They went better, and I did move on to follow-up interviews, but no offer came.

When I arrived home for the Christmas holidays halfway through my senior year, one of our neighbors, Mr. Ted Doty, called me one day. (My mom had mentioned to him that I would soon graduate and was looking for a job.) Mr. Doty was, at the time, manager of corporate accounting operations for GE in Schenectady. His operation audited and reported all the financial information of every business unit in the company.

One of his roles was to interview candidates for the company's Financial Management Training Program. Every year, GE hired about 25 college graduates at the Schenectady plant to go through this three-year program, considered GE's internal MBA program. It was a career path toward becoming potentially one of GE's chief financial officers in one of its 350 businesses around the world.

I had known Mr. Doty since I was eight years old, and I always appreciated his friendliness. When I was growing up, I didn't know he had this position at GE. When he called that day, he said, "Billy, I'd like to talk with you about considering a financial career with GE. I'd like to talk to you about our training program here in the company."

Although I knew the position was located at the Schenectady plant—not my preferred choice—I decided to take the interview because of my admiration for Mr. Doty.

On the day I interviewed, I think my mom was more excited than I was because I'd be close to home. Her coaching was hilarious. "Don't angle your head down. Look him in the eye. Don't chew gum. Give him a firm handshake"...and many more coaching tips made me chuckle. It was the typical type of encouragement my mom always gave me. Though I sometimes felt irritated by it, I also appreciated it then...and later.

The interview was a full day. I met with several people who worked in accounting. Mr. Doty put me right at ease and told me about all the people I would meet. The morning interviews got better and better, and I began to realize by the kinds of questions they were asking that character and confidence were very important. My interviewers wanted to evaluate my level of enthusiasm and interest in working at GE.

At lunch, Mr. Doty asked another manager who worked for him to join us. We dined at the Mohawk Golf Club, a rather elite country club where many GE senior managers had memberships. As we sat down, I admit I remembered my mom's advice. I put on my polite face and remembered the many table manners that she and others had taught me over the years. The waitress asked first if she could take our drink order, and the two older men both looked at me first. I was taken aback and didn't know what to do for a moment. I decided to order an ice tea. To my surprise, they both ordered vodka martinis on the rocks! I questioned whether or not I'd made the right choice, but I could tell from their facial expressions that I had.

That afternoon, when we got back from lunch, I met with Mr. Lou Van Dyck, senior vice president of corporate accounting and Mr. Doty's boss. Mr. Van Dyck was short in stature—about 5'2" or 5'3" with a short crew cut and a colorful bow tie, his signature look. To my surprise, he also was an alumnus of Rutgers and knew Mr. Sahloff. And like me, he'd been student manager of the lacrosse team. We shared many stories about the Rutgers campus, his fraternity, and our great experience at the school. He told me what he expected from all the people who worked for him. I felt like I was in the presence of a teacher or a mentor—someone who showed sincere interest in me.

After I met with him, and again with Mr. Doty, I realized GE was a company I'd be proud to work for. Throughout the interview process, I realized they wanted to know more about what made me tick, what motivated me, and what I wanted to accomplish during my life—a stark contrast to my first job interview on campus.

After I left, I still had to wait a few days to find out if I was hired. Eventually the offer came. The position paid an annual salary of $7,500, which sounded like a lot of money to me. I was very excited, but Mom and Dad were even more so. It was another moment in their lives as parents when they felt all their sacrifices and all the time they'd invested in me had paid off. It was a great validation of their encouragement and support.

I started as a GE financial management trainee in June 1967. Mr. Doty and Mr. Van Dyck asked me to start calling them Ted and Lou. That was the first adjustment I had to make in the business world.

I was a businessman now. I'd made the grade. It was the start of a long, happy, and successful career.

But before I made the transition into the business world, graduation commencement at Rutgers in June 1967 was a day of celebration for my parents. Dad even opened up and expressed his emotions—smiling, beaming with pride, and putting his arm around me. Mom kept smiling all day. My brother, Dick, surprised me and came for the ceremony. It was the first time in years that all four of us celebrated together—a moment I'll always cherish.

THE MOST BEAUTIFUL
GIRL IN THE WORLD

I'd hoped I'd meet the woman I would marry at college. But Rutgers was an all-male school at the time. Enrollment at Rutgers outnumbered enrollment at the all-female school, Douglass College, on the other side of town, eight to one. Rutgers juniors and seniors, in part because they had cars, usually got dates with Douglass coeds. But with my role of student manager of two sports and with Glee Club practices and concerts, time and opportunities to meet girls were limited.

One of my best friends was a star football player and a fraternity brother. He had a car and, one day between football practices, we drove to the Douglass campus and saw two attractive coeds moving all their belongings into their apartment. Like two gallant guys, we asked if they needed help, and they were flattered. We had a fun time helping.

My friend asked one of them to be his date at the first varsity football game against Princeton. I asked the roommate, and she surprised me by saying "yes." We dated several times, which certainly increased my confidence. She was very attractive, fun to be with, and could have gone out with anyone. Dating helped me realize that my physical appearance shouldn't be a concern—that I should simply be myself.

During college, I tagged along with brothers who had cars and connected me with dates. Phi Gamma Delta, the fraternity I joined, was known for its great parties. More importantly, we were known as "gentlemen jocks," and girls enjoyed themselves at our events. Our housemother, Mrs. Lumpkin, made sure of that.

As in high school, I rarely had multiple dates with the same girl. I honestly didn't think about whether my physical appearance affected my ability to develop a long-term relationship. Although the dates were usually fun, I didn't feel a strong attraction to anyone to pursue it further. I was a bit envious of brothers having steady girlfriends or getting engaged. But I didn't need a steady girlfriend to be happy at that stage in my life. I was simply too busy with football, Glee Club, and keeping up with my studies.

When I started working at GE in 1967, many of the other management trainees were married. Those of us who were single went out some nights to grab a pizza or go to a bar to meet, discuss our day, and dance. Schenectady, however, was not a hotbed for nighttime activity, and many of the bars downtown didn't attract singles.

I wasn't comfortable hanging out at bars, anyway, or trying to start up a conversation with a stranger. I wasn't much of a conversationalist. I'd generally be the first person in the group to leave and head home. I envied my married co-workers who headed home every night to wives and, in some cases, children.

My dream was to find a woman with whom I could share my life, have children, and emulate the family experience I'd had growing up. I didn't think that would be difficult. But, as it turned out, it took far longer than I'd imagined. Because I wasn't into the bar scene, or much of a party-goer, my ability to meet women was limited. It was further complicated when I moved into sales, which involved traveling extensively. With the travel, and job changes and promotions that required relocation every two years on average, I didn't establish a network of close friends or get involved in any social groups where I lived.

My first relocation, in sales, was a job in St. Louis in late 1969. I was starting to feel lonely. This first sales job at GE meant I covered and had to travel a four-state area by car. I spent many hours on the road and on my own. While I didn't mind being alone and learning to be content on my own, that wasn't how I wanted to live my life.

By the early '70s, I began to question whether I'd ever meet someone with whom I could share my life. I was growing impatient, even though I was only in my mid-20s. The thought of being single the rest of my life began to drag me down. Even the thought that women found me unattractive, given my disabilities, crept back into my mind.

In 1972, I accepted an opportunity at GE's Silicone Products Division in Waterford, New York, not far from Schenectady. I took a position working for the sales manager of that business as his sales administrator. That position enabled me to interact with all sales personnel who worked in offices across the country. I attended many sales meetings that included evening social events. I met women who worked as customer service representatives in most of the sales offices, but many were either married, dating someone, or much older than me. There were very few single women at headquarters where I worked. My prospects didn't look promising.

In the early spring of 1973, I accepted a promotion to become the customer service manager for the division. In addition to managing the headquarters operation, I worked with the customer service reps in all our offices scattered across the country. Soon I had met all of them at regional sales meetings, with the exception of the reps in our West Coast office, located in the Los Angeles area. The main rep in that office was Kathy Walsh. My only interaction with her was over the phone, discussing inventory shipments and other issues. I had heard from co-workers that she was good-looking and single.

In the summer of '73, she spent a week on vacation back east with a girlfriend who happened to work for me. Kathy decided to visit the plant, meet me, and say hello to others in our group. We didn't spend a lot of time together that time, but I found her attractive and very friendly.

In October, I held a meeting at the plant for the customer service reps from around the country—to introduce them to a new, computerized order-entry system. In addition to our daytime meetings, there were evening social events. I had heard that Kathy's birthday was on the first night, and I ordered a cake to celebrate.

On the final evening of our meeting, a group of us went out dancing. It was the night that changed my life forever.

I knew that I wanted to dance with Kathy. She was attractive, and had such a bright smile, beautiful eyes, and an outgoing personality. I could tell she was a happy person. We danced many times that evening.

On that night, I fell in love with Kathy, and I sensed she felt the same way. At the end of the evening, I walked her back to her room and kissed her good night. She flew back to Los Angeles the next morning.

We began talking daily by phone. I'd actually call to wake her up in the morning (I was three hours ahead on the East Coast). GE had WATS phone lines, so I'd also call Kathy after 5 p.m., because calls from our office after that time didn't affect the company's phone costs. We often talked in the evenings and during the weekends. I felt so comfortable talking to her, as if I had known her for many years.

Our relationship progressed very quickly after the training session. My 10th high-school reunion was the next month, in November, and I invited her back for that and to meet my parents. Mom kept asking me, "Why couldn't you meet a girl from around here?" Kathy's sister asked her, "Why couldn't you meet a man in California—why so far away?" After spending more time with each other that reunion weekend, we decided that if we were going to pursue our relationship we needed to be together, in the same town.

Kathy decided to make the move to New York. Through a mutual GE friend and manager, she was hired for a customer service rep position in another nearby GE business. She found an apartment about a mile from mine. It was a major decision on her part—leaving a good job and moving 3,000 miles away.

Soon we knew that our love for each other was real, and we were both ready for marriage. I was 28, Kathy was 27. Kathy had gone through the same feelings of loneliness and was beginning to think she might remain single. I wanted to live with her for the rest of my life. She was an outgoing, attractive woman who showed genuine care and love for others. On May 25, 1974, we became husband and wife.

Shortly before I met her, Kathy had become a born-again Christian, committing her life to Christ in December 1971. Taking that step had dramatically changed her life. My faith journey was a little different. I'd grown up going regularly to church, attending Sunday school and youth group, and believing in God. But I'd categorize my faith as alive but dormant when I met Kathy.

Kathy encouraged me to grow significantly in my faith. She helped me understand the importance of having a close relationship with Christ and understanding His promise of salvation. I had always put my faith in my own abilities and my dependence on other people, such as my parents. She helped me realize that my faith, trust, and dependence on Him were what I needed to build upon.

We're approaching our 40th wedding anniversary and I'm just as much, if not more, in love with Kathy now as when I first met her. Making God the center of our marriage has kept it strong and vibrant, and kept the commitment strong.

'YOU HAVE NO IDEA'

After my father died in 1987, my mom was on her own in her home for several years. A series of falls made her decide to sell her house and move into an assisted-living facility. Before her move, she needed help deciding which belongings to keep.

Mom at age 80 with a keepsake (my batting stance photo)

My wife, Kathy, offered to help and flew back to Schenectady. Mom appreciated Kathy's assistance and company as they went through boxes of pictures and other items that brought back many memories. It was a special time they shared.

In 1995, at the age of 85, Mom experienced a stroke and had to be hospitalized. She had suffered minor strokes several times before—strokes so small that they didn't limit her functioning. During her hospital stay, I kept in touch with her regularly by phone (from Wisconsin to New York), and she always steered the conversation toward me. "How are the kids?" she asked, "Is the business going OK?" "Are you taking care of yourself?" and "I worry about you." Several times I told her I'd like to come visit her, but she said, "No, I'm OK. Just save your money. Please, you don't need to come."

In September 1995, I called her hospital room regularly. On one of those days when I called, a nurse answered instead of Mom. I told her who I was. She hesitated a bit, and then said, "I'm sorry to tell you that your mom passed away this morning."

I was numb. I really didn't know what to do or say. I left my office and took a walk, and a feeling of guilt overcame me. I should have visited her even if it was against her wishes. I'd had a chance to tell her one more time how much I appreciated her for what she had done for me.

Now that chance was gone. A feeling of deep sadness overwhelmed me. The person who had brought me into this world, who had the greatest impact on my life, and who represented my happiness, was gone.

But as I walked further, and uncontrollable tears kept coming, I realized Mom wouldn't want me to feel that way. She knew I appreciated her and loved her, and I realized I needed to continue to honor her by the way I lived my life.

When Kathy had visited her and Mom had reminisced and shared stories, Kathy said she'd often pause and reflect on this trial or that experience regarding raising me. She'd occasionally look up and say many times, "You have no idea." But she certainly wasn't complaining. Raising me was a monumental challenge over many years, and she faced obstacle after obstacle in determining and meeting my physical and emotional needs. No hurdle Mom faced during those years was simple or straightforward.

It would have been easier for her if she'd sheltered me and not allowed me to be so active. A less active life would have helped her avoid the many needed replacements and repairs of my artificial limb. No one would have criticized my parents if they had made my life simple by limiting my physical activities.

But from the day I was born, Mom was determined to raise me as a normal child. She made a conscious decision to expose me to the many things any young boy would be interested in. Beyond any safety considerations, there would be no limits. She allowed me to discover and develop my own interests and, at the same time, exposed me to new experiences she felt I could handle. Aunt Mickey certainly helped and encouraged her to let me "try." She wanted me to have as many opportunities as possible.

The reality was that my parents faced unknown territory when I was born. The questions must have been overwhelming:

- Where do we go and who can we talk to about his deformed leg?
- Will he be able to use his left arm and hand?
- How and when will we get him fitted for an artificial limb?
- Could an artificial leg be designed for his condition?
- How will he learn to walk with one?
- What will happen as he continues to grow?
- How can we afford to make this all happen?
- Can we get any financial help?
- What about the clothes that will need constant alterations?
- How far do we let him go when he wants to participate in a physical activity?

Those were some of the very practical questions for which they needed answers. But they also wondered about my emotional needs, how to meet them, and how to encourage me as I faced many challenges.

Mom was unfailing in her love and encouragement, and the many, many sacrifices she made. In all my years growing up, we never had any discussion that included the word "can't." She never looked at me and said, "You're handicapped," or "You have a disability." We both knew I faced particular challenges, but we never dwelled on them.

Mom let me try more and more activities as she realized my adaptability, and the happiness I experienced in trying new things. She introduced me to music. She let me play sports, even though it led to broken parts in my leg and many trips to the brace-maker. She and Dad let me try out for Little League, and the school basketball and baseball teams. And they nurtured my interest in the game of golf.

While my self-confidence grew as I met new challenges, sometimes the challenges seemed too difficult. But by trying, I succeeded. I'm sure in private Mom worried about me—asking herself questions like, "Will he hurt himself?" "Will he get discouraged if, or when, he fails?" "Am I being a good mom by letting him try things where he could potentially get hurt or, more likely, not succeed?

Mom kept those worries and concerns to herself, and never let me know those doubts.

I also had so many practical needs that were above and beyond the norm. From the day I was born and throughout my childhood, Mom sewed and altered my clothes to fit my deformed arm and leg. The left arm length on shirts and outerwear had to be shortened, underwear had to be altered to conform to my right stump, and my pant leg length was different for my legs. I was also born with a very small foot, which required finding a make of shoe that fit.

All these alterations were ongoing as I grew in size and was fitted for new artificial legs. I never heard Mom complain about any of these things. She always put me first, ahead of her own needs.

Mom didn't want people to treat me as "special." All through my school years, she helped me learn how to get along with other kids, and to respect my teachers and authority. At times when my grades dipped, my parents sat me down and told me I needed to improve. A few times, I acted up and found myself in the principal's office. When Mom had to come to school to pick me up, I learned there were consequences for my actions. She gave me very little grace when I misbehaved. At some points, I thought of my parents as being mean. But because they treated me like anyone else, I was raised like a normal boy. I learned the importance of respect for others, humility, and responsibility.

My parents sacrificed so many things for me. I know my situation put financial stress on them, and they had to forego things they would have liked to have done. They had to be very careful with their finances. They had to continually save for my new legs, which had to be replaced and repaired regularly. And they saved for the college education they wanted me to have.

Mom and Dad, my great encouragers (1982)

My parents' example of putting me first ahead of their own wants shaped my attitude about life. As a parent, I've tried to emulate their example, and I've always wanted to serve other people when I can.

Because of their great example, my parents were the first ones I'd go to when I accomplished something. I wanted them to know my love for them by sharing my successes. I wanted them to know they played a big part in it. I couldn't do it alone.

Those words my mom uttered—"You have no idea"—describe the challenges my parents faced and the sacrifices they made in raising me. If they were alive today, they'd say it was all worth it. They'd say that the joy they experienced when they saw me succeed was a blessing for them. That's the kind of caring people they were. And they saw the end result—their son's happy and fulfilling life.

LOOKING BACK

Writing this book has given me the opportunity to reflect on my life and the people who were a significant part of it. Looking back has given me a renewed appreciation for the challenging journey I've taken; the trials and triumphs that have made me the person I am today. One word that constantly pops into my mind defines my life.

That word is "acceptance."

I came into this world facing many challenges I couldn't overcome on my own. I could not have done it without the aid and encouragement of others. Even when I was old enough to live and think independently, there were people in my life who helped and guided me. In any given moment, it's easy to think we can accomplish things and make the right decisions on our own, without anyone's help. But looking back at the path I've walked, there was always someone beside me, helping me, even when I didn't feel I needed it.

It all started with my parents who, from the moment they saw me, accepted me the way I was. Their mission was to raise me like any other child, and to allow me to pursue any opportunities I was interested in. They faced so many difficult decisions with no previous experience dealing with a child with disabilities. They brought me through a very challenging period in my life, which was a monumental challenge for them, as well.

Their show of love to me gave me security, even during those long periods at the hospital when we were separated. They insulated me from the stress and anguish they were feeling as they faced hurdle after hurdle, decision after decision, in making sure I could face the physical and emotional demands of life. They constantly encouraged me to "try" and to feel good about it, no matter the outcome. They recognized the will I had to overcome obstacles. They saw me persist, take another step, and then another. They saw me fall, but let me get up and try again.

I must single out my mother as the one who guided me the most during my childhood. Certainly Dad loved me and provided for us, but it was Mom who was the caregiver, the nurturer, the encourager.

My mom sacrificed her life for me and gave me the guidance and direction, the praise and support, and the love that created in me a healthy sense of self-confidence.

For obvious reasons, Mom was hesitant about allowing me to take on physical activities and challenges. She was concerned about my safety and didn't want me to get discouraged if I couldn't handle them. But she wouldn't let my disability define me or hold me back. She knew I had the ability and confidence to try new things, and she didn't keep them from me—even though it might have made her life much calmer and simpler. I could not and would not have traveled this life path without the encouragement, sacrifice, and love from my mom.

Aunt Mickey certainly helped both Mom and me. She saw my desire and determination to try activities, like swimming and golf, and she encouraged my mom to let me try. She took the lead in teaching me these sports, which helped Mom immensely. Aunt Mickey saw my coordination and knew I could succeed. Aunt Mickey was my first "coach"—always getting me to try. In the few times I was down on myself, she was there to pick me up and help me turn my attitude around.

Aunt Mickey, my great "coach," and Mom; with Dad
and Uncle Teen behind them (March 1980)

Many childhood friends also made a difference in my life. They
didn't ignore me or treat me like an outsider. The other guys my age easily
could have excluded or isolated me if they'd judged me on my physical
appearance. My buddies always included me in any neighborhood and
school games. I know my athletic ability helped me to be accepted. The
guys saw me hitting and catching baseballs, shooting baskets, throwing
footballs, swimming, bowling, and playing golf. They were amazed at
how much I could do and how well I could do it.

Being able to play sports and keep up with all of them also helped
me develop lasting friendships. In my neighborhood in Schenectady,
I was "just one of the kids." We played together, fought together, and
stayed together as friends. We competed hard—with and against
each other—and developed close-knit friendships. Jimmy Emery, in
particular, was a great friend. We grew up together. From the time we
were very young, we spent many hours together each day.

A couple of years ago—50-plus years after first meeting each other—we reconnected. I visited Jim (not Jimmy anymore) and his wife in Savannah, Georgia. Another neighborhood buddy, Jack Lauroesch, joined us. We simply picked up where we left off—revisiting old times, playing a few rounds of golf, and looking at old photographs, which led to lots of laughter. Both Jim and Jack commented on how I was just one of the gang, and they never considered me handicapped.

The friends I made in junior high and high school are too numerous to mention by name, and I so appreciate their acceptance of me. Recently, an old high-school friend and I were discussing school memories, reminiscing about our time together on the basketball team. He was one of the best outside shooters on our team. While the team practiced. I was on the sidelines shooting free throws when I wasn't needed in my role as student manager.

At the end of each practice, the coach would have a free-throw shooting contest, and he always included me. My friend reminded me that in most of the contests it came down to him and me as the final two, and he remembered me beating him most of the time. He said everyone just considered me "one of the guys."

"To us," he said, "you were no different than anyone else. We never considered you handicapped." Being "just one of the guys" is one of the greatest gifts in my life.

I recently returned to Schenectady for our 50th high-school reunion. As we all gathered the first night to share stories, warm memories came over me—seeing and talking to my former high-school classmates who'd made my high-school experience one of the happiest times in my life.

My many coaches through the years found a place on their teams for me after seeing my love for sports, admiring my determination and competitiveness, and witnessing my positive attitude. To them, I was an important member of the team, not a charity case. And I learned so much by observing them as coaches and leaders and from the life lessons they taught us:

- The importance and ability to be humble in victory and gracious in defeat;
- The desire and determination to do your best for your team and teammates; and
- The importance of depending on each other, and doing your personal best.

These skills—perseverance, hard work, belief in self, ability to handle adversity, teamwork—are all lessons I took into my life as an adult and as a businessman. I was able to experience all of this because I was included. I was accepted.

Throughout my college experience at Rutgers, I had even more opportunities—as a member of the football and lacrosse teams, the Glee Club, and the Phi Gamma Delta fraternity chapter. I developed many close friendships from these experiences. Those friends now are scattered across the country. Many have retired or have passed away. But the times spent with them will remain fresh in my mind. I'll always remember our times together and the part they played in my life journey.

The same is true of all the friends I've made in the business world, particularly during the time I worked at GE. Most of my years with the company were spent in the silicone products group. The many friendships I made there are still strong to this day. Some of us get together in Myrtle Beach every year for a few days of golf and a lot of time sharing memories. Though we worked together more than 30 years ago, the bond is strong. And, of course, GE is where I found the wife of my dreams.

Kathy has been a wonderful wife and a constant encouragement to me since 1974, when we married. She easily could have picked other men to share her life with, but she picked me. She told me one thing that attracted her to me was the love I showed for my mom. Kathy is definitely the woman I dreamed about marrying—a beautiful, caring woman who always puts the interests of others ahead of her own. Kathy and Mom are a lot alike in that regard. Kathy also helped me grow spiritually and helped me realize the need for a closer relationship with God. She showed me the importance of putting my faith and trust in Him.

During our many years living in Madison, Wisconsin, Kathy and I have developed genuine relationships with great friends—in our neighborhoods and in our churches. To top it off, we've been blessed with children and grandchildren.

For me, one group of men has been a particularly strong influence on me. They have truly enriched my life. They've helped me grow spiritually, and as a man. We socialize, worship, and pray for each other, and we hold each other accountable in our lives. We're truly brothers in so many ways.

Acceptance from my parents and acceptance from my friends: These are great gifts that I open and enjoy every day of my life.

But there's one other person in my life, the most important one, who has loved and accepted me since I was conceived—Jesus Christ, God's only Son. He looks upon me as perfect and always has. He created me the way He wanted me to be. He suffered and died for me—for us all—and paid the price, in full, for our sins. He has carried my burdens, walked beside me, never letting me walk alone. The extent of His love and acceptance came shining through as I looked back at my life, my journey, and the people He brought into my life along the way.

Some people have called me courageous. That would mean I did it on my own. But I couldn't have made this journey without the help and encouragement of so many people in my life. I was blessed with the will and determination to overcome, but it would have withered and died without the support of others.

I did not and could not do it alone.

How can I account for the people who've come into my life and the timing and circumstances that led to their involvement? As human beings, we tend to think we were "in the right place at the right time," or that we "couldn't have timed it any better," or "what a coincidence" when people or situations become part of our lives.

But it's clear to me that God has created the path I have lived. He:

- Gave me two parents who loved and encouraged me and who had the confidence to raise me the way they did;
- Connected them with medical people who gave them hope and guidance;
- Pulled me through a very dark time in the hospital;
- Put us in the right neighborhoods, the right schools, and gave me teachers and coaches who supported me;
- Gave me interest in and ability in several sports, my passion, which built up my self-confidence and self-esteem;
- Surrounded me with friends throughout my life who've included and accepted me;
- Opened up doors through other people that made my college education possible;
- Placed me in the right jobs to build a career;
- Brought Kathy and me together in an amazing way;
- Enabled me to be a leader in my church and my community, so I could "give back" and help others; and
- Gave me the opportunity to be a father and a grandfather.

Who else but God could have orchestrated it all—the people, the timing, and the circumstances? It's an easy decision for me to put my faith and trust in Him, to thank him for His grace and mercy, and to recognize his unfailing love.

Looking back, I see that God made many wonderful things possible. And He still does.

ABOUT THE AUTHOR

Bill & Kathy Schultz

Bill Schultz has owned and managed an executive search firm in Madison, Wisconsin for more than 25 years.

Bill has long been active in his community as a Little League coach and ministry leader in his church. He volunteers in community organizations, including the American Family Children's Hospital.

He lives in Madison with his wife, Kathy. They have two grown children – Brian and Bethany – and two granddaughters.

He's a motivational/inspirational speaker on the topics of encouragement and overcoming life obstacles. He feels called to speak on this topic to audiences of parents of children with special needs and to school-age children of all abilities.

"My goal is to share my personal story as an example of how acceptance and encouragement from others can positively impact one's life. It started with loving parents. I faced major physical challenges from the time I was born. I was different from the other kids in my neighborhood and at school. Instead of being picked on or bullied, I was accepted by my friends and schoolmates. The healthy self-confidence and self-esteem that resulted from that has enabled me to live a life of fulfillment."

For speaking engagements:
    – Please contact him at bschultz7782@gmail.com.

CPSIA information can be obtained at www.ICGtesting.com
Printed in the USA
LVOW06s1911100414

381198LV00002B/5/P